Books by R. D. Rosen

*Me and My Friends, We No Longer Profess
Any Graces:* A Premature Memoir   1971

Psychobabble   1977

PSYCHOBABBLE

PSYCHO

*Fast Talk and Quick Cure
in the Era of Feeling*

BABBLE

R. D. ROSEN

NEW YORK   1977   *Atheneum*

Library of Congress Cataloging in Publication Data
Rosen, Richard Dean, 1949–
  Psychobabble.
  Bibliography: p.
  1. Psychotherapy. I. Title.
  RC480.R665   158   77-76465
  ISBN 0-689-10775-7

The chapters entitled "Psychobabble" and "Computer Therapy:
Please Continue, This May Be Interesting" first appeared in slightly
different form in *New Times*. The chapter entitled *"est:* The Self
Is Fun to the Self" first appeared in slightly different form in *The
Boston Phoenix.*

for Diane

ACKNOWLEDGMENTS

Thanks especially to Robert Crosby, Charles Dawe and William F. Murphy for their ideas, indulgence, criticism and support; and I am extremely grateful to all of the following, who offered support in many forms at various stages of the book's completion: James Atlas, Peter Birge, David Bloom, Sidney Blumenthal, Tony Chase, Ben Gerson, Russell Jacoby, Judith Kern, Joanna Krotz, Frank Rich, Erica Spellman, and my parents, brothers and sister.

INTRODUCTION

I n 1972, another journalist and I conceived a small plot. The weekly newspaper we worked for was at that particular stage in its growth open to harmless pranks, and we decided to invent a cult in western Massachusetts in order to write a feature story about it. We called our imaginary commune Sansuki and, thinking to spoof the various cults that had recently won the attention of the mass media, reported that the communards were involved in trying to reach two states on the spiritual continuum. The first was the state of vegetable consciousness, called Brachli, the second a state described in neurophysiological gibberish as a regression to the primacy of the rhinencephalon, or reptile brain.

Although the story contained several believable anecdotes, we thought we had been careful to include enough ludicrous details to make clear our intentions. There was the ethereal ex-medical student and now commune leader named "bob," known also as the "head lettuce." There were scenes of violence among vegetarians and one of a woman curled up into a ball pretending she was a tomato. But our joke was more successful than we had ever imagined. Not only did the newspaper receive a handful of letters asking soberly for more information about Sansuki, but even members of the newspaper staff, perhaps already numbed by front page lunacy, were surprised to discover that such a place did not, in fact, exist. (One reader, to our relief, did write a clever letter to say that, as a member of Sansuki, he appreciated the fairness with which we had treated the cult.)

We were amused and slightly alarmed by what appeared to be a ripening public credulity regarding psychological and spiritual pursuits. Something was clearly in the air. A couple of years later, when I had turned to a more serious interest in psychology, something was still in the air. I was trying to make sense of the bewildering proliferation of self-improvement manuals and popular psychotherapies, some of the latter as bizarre at first glance as Sansuki. A manic, self-regarding, relentlessly psychological atmosphere had developed. I was both an observer of it and, by virtue of my very interest in human growth, also a participant.

While I was composing a book review in 1975, the word "psychobabble" materialized on the page and suddenly I had a term to describe a particular cultural climate. This book, which grew out of that word, is my own effort to depict and interpret some of the therapeutic trends of the seventies. The therapies with which this book concerns itself are only a sample of those available and not the only ones that could have illustrated the significant aspects of psychobabble, but they have been chosen with an eye toward capturing some of the most interesting features of contemporary psychological pre-occupations.

In any case, this book is not intended as a survey, even of those therapies discussed at length. The issues addressed here go beyond considerations of who can find what kind of happiness where. My judgments of the therapies are, of course, reflections in part of my own psychological and political disposition but, more important, those judgments are generally made in the service of a broader theme: the relationship between language and psychology and the subversion of that relationship by the jargon of the day.

The names and identities of some of the people in the book have been changed.

CONTENTS

PSYCHOBABBLE

PSYCHOBABBLE

WHILE HAVING DRINKS a couple of years ago with a young woman I had not seen for some time, I asked how things were going and received this reply: "I've really been getting in touch with myself lately. I've struck some really deep chords." I winced at the grandeur of her remarks, but she proceeded, undaunted, to reel out a string of broad psychological insights with an enthusiasm attributable less to the Tequila Sunrise sitting before her than to the confessional spirit sweeping America.

I kept thinking I was disappointing her with my failure to introduce more lyricism and intensity into my own conversation. Now that circumspection and reticence had gone out of style, I felt obligated to reciprocate her candor but couldn't bring myself to use the popular catchphrases of revelation.

Would she understand if I said that instead of striking deep chords I had merely tickled the ivories of my psychic piano? That getting my head together was not exactly the way in which I wished to describe the sensation from my neck up? Would it, I wondered, do any good if I resorted to more precise clinical language and admitted that I was well on the way to resolving my attitude toward my maternal introject?

"Whenever I see you," she said brightly, "it makes me feel so good inside. It's a real high-energy experience."

So what was wrong with me that I couldn't feel the full voltage of our contact? Unable to match her incandescence, I muttered, "Yes, it's good to see you," then fell silent.

Finally, she said, her beatific smile widening, "But I can really dig your silence. If you're bummed out, that's okay."

If anything characterizes the cultural life of the seventies in America, it is an insistence on preventing failures of communication. Everything must now be spoken. The Kinsey report, Masters and Johnson, *The Joy of Sex* and its derivatives; the *Playboy Advisor*, the *Penthouse Forum*, *Oui's Sex Tapes*; contraception; the Esalen ethos and the human potential movement; the democratization of psychotherapy; the suspicion that technology and imperialism have rendered us incapable of something called "feeling," a shortcoming everyone is aggressively engaged in correcting—all these various oils have helped lubricate the national tongue. It's as if the full bladder of civilization's squeamishness had burst (though hardly for the first time). The sexual revolution, this therapeutic age, has culminated in one profuse, steady stream of self-revelation, confessed profligacy, and publicized domestic and intrapsychic trauma.

It seems that everyone belongs to the cult of candor these days and that everyone speaks the same dialect. Are you relating? Good. Are you getting in touch with yourself? Fine.

4

Exactly how heavy are those changes you're going through? Doing your own thing? (Or are you, by some mistake, doing someone else's?) Is your head screwed on straight? Are you going to get your act together, or just your shit? Are you mind-fucked, or just engaged in cortical foreplay? Are you a whole person or only a fraction thereof?

One hears it everywhere, like endless panels of a Jules Feiffer cartoon. In restaurants, distraught lovers lament, "I just wish I could get into your head." A man on a bus turns to his companion and says, "I just got back from the Coast. What a different headset!" The latest reports from a declining Esalen provide us with new punch lines: a group leader there intones that "it's beautiful if you're unhappy. Go with the feeling. . . . You gotta be you 'cause you're you and you gotta be, and besides, if you aren't gonna be you who else's gonna be you, honey? . . . This is the Aquarian Age and the time to be yourself, to love one's beauty, to go with one's process."

It's apparent that we can't proceed any further without a name for this institutionalized garrulousness, this psychological patter, this need to catalogue the ego's condition. Let's call it psychobabble, this spirit which now tyrannizes conversation in the seventies. Psychobabble is difficult to avoid and there is often an embarrassment involved in not using it, somewhat akin to the mild humiliation experienced by American tourists in Paris who cannot speak the native tongue. Psychobabble is now spoken by magazine editors, management consultants, sandal makers, tool and die workers, chiefs of state, Ph.D.s in clinical psychology, and just about everyone else.

In the sixties, sociologist Philip Rieff developed a theory about "Psychological Man," the dominant mid-twentieth-century figure who, finding traditional sorts of faith no longer useful, turned to himself under the auspices of modern psy-

chology. He became a victim of his own interminable introspection, and acquired the belief that "a sense of well-being
has become the end, rather than a by-product of striving
after some superior communal end." The idea of a new style
of human being, one whose existence is geared to the avoidance of affliction, became evident even at the end of the last
century, as historian Donald Meyer has pointed out. But this
Psychological Man has regressed in the seventies to an adolescent—not just the victim of interminable introspection
but also the victim of his own inability to describe human
behavior with anything but platitudes. One psychoanalyst,
who has observed the ascendancy of therapeutic interest over
the course of several decades, takes its measure in the fact
that "virtually everyone who is touched by psychoanalysis
identifies with it and soon wants to become a therapist himself. Eventually there will be one fantastic group, like a
therapeutic chain letter. Ultimately, all these different therapies will look the same and everyone will say 'Fuck it' and
then get back to the basics, like how to feed the world."

Yes, but until then we have psychobabble. Its more
specific origins can perhaps only be hinted at. On one level,
it seems to have emerged toward the end of the sixties, dis-
tilled from the dying radical/liberal dialects of activism and
confrontation, absorbing some black ghetto phrases along the
way. But its roots are also firmly planted in the language of
the human potential movement with its Fritz Perls of wisdom. One of psychobabble's problems is its insistence on
interpreting the individual's history and history in general as
the result of *conscious* choices; in this, psychobabble has fed
both on the tendency toward shallow political analysis and
sloganeering that was certainly one feature of the sixties
counterculture as well as on the human potential movement
with its emphasis on ego psychology at the expense of a
deeper, psychodynamic critique.

6

Political activism was acquiring more and more of a therapeutic cast toward the end of the sixties, particularly as the left fragmented and the great communal causes splintered into smaller, more idiosyncratic crusades. Many radical battles, once fought exclusively in the real political world, were now being enacted in the individual psyche. T-groups, encounter groups, sensitivity training, group gropes, psychodrama, and primal scream therapies (this last an apt reflection of the clamorous sixties) all helped return political conflicts to the realm of the personal. Four years ago, when Jerry Rubin proclaimed in *Psychology Today* that he was going back to his body, where the real wars of liberation were taking place, those who hadn't already preceded him now rushed to swap their exhausted political ambitions for therapeutic ideals (in the interim, Rubin attached himself to almost all the newest therapies and became a media-circuit spokesman for a new "love and peace" message stripped of its former political content). Somewhere along the line—it is hard to remember just when—the disaffected were saying "Off the pigs!" one day and "Man, I'm really tense, don't mess with my head" the next.

On another level, the emergence of psychobabble is a provisional and highly imperfect solution to the problem of what sort of language to use to describe feeling states, behavior, and emotional growth. Looked at in this way, psychobabble can be seen as a feeble compromise between two contending visions of human behavior. First, there are the behaviorists, who see human behavior as *causal* and psychology as an empirical science. Their stimulus-response paradigm reduces us to the status of rats (if we ever do end up acting just like rats or Pavlov's dogs, it will be largely because behaviorism has conditioned us to do so) and makes any talk of feelings or unconscious mental life largely irrelevant. According to behaviorists, the only things that count in human behavior are those that can be observed. Hence the joke about two behaviorists who meet at a convention: "You look like you're doing fine," says one. "How am I doing?" But, of course, behaviorists point out the fallacy of their own theory by their very existence; as Walker Percy remarks in *The Message in the Bottle*, ". . . after all the behavior of behaviorists is notable in that it is not encompassed by behavioral theory: behaviorists not only study responses; they write articles and deliver lectures setting forth what they take to be the truth about responses, and would be offended if anyone suggested that their writings and lectures were nothing more than responses and therefore no more true or false than a dog's salivation." Behaviorists have trouble, then, paying homage to their own beliefs. One Arnold Lazarus recounted in a *Psychological Reports* article how he sought to arrange a meeting of leading behavior therapists, but was stunned to find that most couldn't attend because of a conflict: the meeting fell on a day when they had appointments with their psychoanalysts.

The second contending vision is the psychoanalytic or psychodynamic theory of behavior—that our actions (thoughts, wishes) don't have causes but rather meanings and motives that arise from a complex play of intrapsychic conflicts and clashes with the environment. Psychoanalytic theory doesn't refute the behaviorists so much as put them in their place as custodians of a *partial* explanation of human behavior. Those who believe in the psychoanalytic perspective see a difficult logic in the richness of human behavior but lack an effective vocabulary for systematizing their insights in ordinary language.

So the language of behaviorism is too arid and that of psychoanalysis too complicated to offer an attractive vocabulary for conversational use. It has fallen to a third general psychological camp—ego psychology and the human potential movement—to do that. This vast category—which includes neo-Freudians like Alfred Adler and Erich Fromm, non-psychoanalytic thinkers like Abraham Maslow and Carl Rogers, as well as the Esalen crowd, for starters—has emphasized the conscious ego as the true subject of psychological theory and practice, and has minimized, or entirely ignored, Freud's most challenging discoveries—the persistence of the unconscious, the interpretation of dreams, the theory of repression. In varying degrees, they are interested in the "here and now" and the possibility of psychological solutions that do not require dwelling on the individual's childhood in order to be effective. Where Freud formulated a psyche forever at war with itself and the culture it inhabits (or, one might say, the culture that inhabits it), the human potential movement speaks relentlessly of a "self" or "the real self" (Karen Horney), "self-actualization" (Maslow), and the "whole person" (Rogers). Where Freud saw a mortgage that could never be entirely paid off, the human potential movement hints at a final freedom and a life lived in the black.

The vocabulary of "self" and "whole person," etc., has installed itself comfortably in popular speech. There is no question but that these words are highly evocative and seem to have a natural place in our verbal picture of the world. But their meanings are so elusive and subject to ad hoc definitions that they have come at last to represent, not a theory or an understanding, but rather just a *style* of speech. They are easy terms to use precisely because they are so adaptable to various meanings, and, for this very reason, they have a way of swallowing up complexities in their large and inelegant folds. Psychobabble is, at least in part, the use of these terms elevated to a fashion of observation.

Of course, this is not the first time in our history that psychological ideas have so dominated national conversation. Previ-

9

ously, in the forties and fifties, Freudian terms gained a vulgar, wholesale currency and were used for intellectual oneupmanship. Freudian terminology was so ardently embraced by liberal magazines, novelists, and the middle class that the growing demand for the thing itself—psychoanalysis—soon outdistanced the supply of doctors. It is interesting to look back at the way in which writers would noisily wheel in their faulty appreciation of Freud in the middle of dialogues, as when Al Manheim, Budd Schulberg's narrator in *What Makes Sammy Run?*, suddenly begins talking about id, ego, and superego and manages to get most of it wrong.

As one Boston psychoanalyst who has practiced for over thirty years says, "After the war, everyone was talking simplistically about the Oedipus complex. It was the rage. Everyone had the idea that knowledge itself would make you free." Now he has to listen to the new psychobabble. A patient of his, a social worker and group leader in his thirties, eagerly responded at the beginning of therapy to each interpretation his analyst made by saying, "I hear you, I hear you."

"I'm sorry," said the doctor, "I didn't know you were a little deaf."

"I'm not. I *hear* you. It means I comprehend."

"Well, what is it that you comprehend?"

The patient paused. "Jesus," he finally replied. "I don't know."

Psychobabble, the psychoanalyst muses, "is just a way of using candor in order not to be candid." The similar dangers of the old psychobabble were remarked on as early as 1929 by another Boston psychoanalyst: "Everybody talks glibly of repression, complexes, sublimation, wish fulfillment and subconsciousness as if they really understood Freud and what he was talking about. Gentle reader, let me say this, that with the exception of a few professional philosophers, psychologists, psychiatrists and psychoanalysts, I have not met a dozen people who knew more than the terms of Freud."

The new psychobabblers, however, don't even seem to know the *terms*—of Freudian or any other organized body of psychological theory. Their jargon seems instead to free-float in an all-purpose linguistic atmosphere, a set of repetitive verbal formalities that kills off the very spontaneity, candor, and understanding it pretends to promote. It's an idiom that reduces psychological insight to a collection of standardized observations, that provides a frozen lexicon to deal with an infinite variety of problems. *Uptight,* for instance, is a word used to describe an individual experiencing anything from mild uneasiness to a clinical depression. To ask someone why he or she refers to another as being *hung-up* elicits a reply that reveals neither understanding nor curiosity: "Well, you know, he's just, well, *hung-up.*" And interestingly, those few psychiatric terms borrowed by psychobabble are used recklessly. One is no longer fearful; one is *paranoid.* The adjective is applied with a generosity that would be confusing to any real clinical paranoiac. Increasingly, people describe their moody acquaintances as *manic-depressives,* and almost anyone you don't like is *psychotic* or at the very least *schizzed-out.*

Many people express the view that this new psychobabble is a constructive retreat from obfuscating clinical terms, but if so, it is only a retreat into a sweet banality, a sort of syrup poured over conversations in order to make them go down easier. Kierkegaard recoiled, in the middle of the nineteenth century, at the false, romanticized candor he sensed about him: "Our age . . . demands, if not lofty then at least loud-voiced pathos, if not speculation then surely results, if not truth then conviction, if not honesty then certainly affidavits to that effect, if not emotion then incessant talk about it." This reminds one of Samuel Johnson's reply when Boswell complained to him, "I have often blamed myself, Sir, for not feeling for others as sensibly as many say they do." "Sir," Johnson said, "don't be duped by them any more. You will find these very feeling people are not very ready to do you good. They *pay* you by *feeling*."

Psychobabble, as a style of speech (as opposed to the jargon of certain specific therapies, which will be discussed in later chapters), is more than anything else a feature of contemporary decorum, a form of politesse, a signal to others that one is ready to talk turkey, to engage in *real dialogue*. Unfortunately, in the rush for revelation, real dialogue often turns out to be real monologue. When I asked a man to whom I had just been introduced at a party recently, "How are you?" (no doubt an early, but harmless, form of psychobabble!), he responded by describing, with an utter disrespect for brevity, his relationship with his wife.

Confession, alas, is the new handshake.

If psychobabble were a question of language alone, the worst one could say about it is that it is just another example of the corrosion of the English language. But the prevalence of psychobabble signifies more than a mere "loss for words." One never loses just words, of course, and so psychobabble represents a loss of understanding and the freedoms that accompany understanding as well.

There has been now for several years a tendency to believe in the ethos of "being oneself" and in the promises of total liberation. This trend has been well-documented in some excellent books during the last ten years. In his recent *Social Amnesia: A Critique of Conformist Psychology from Adler to Laing*, social historian Russell Jacoby noted that the reasons for this current occupation with self and liberation go beyond the *voluntary* desire to be enlightened: "The more the development of late capitalism renders obsolete or at least suspect the real possibilities of self, self-fulfillment and actualization, the more they are emphasized as if they could spring to life through an act of will alone." If Jacoby is right, and I think he is, then psychobabble must be seen as the expression not of a victory over dehumanization but as its latest and very subtle victory over us. What the casual use of psychobabble accomplishes is this: it transforms self-understanding, which each must gain gradually through experience and analysis, into tokens of self-understanding that can be exchanged between people, but without any clear psychological value.

Psychobabble facilitates a belief in the immediate availability of well-being. I once spoke with a young woman at an Erhard Seminars Training guest lecture who, after three years of relatively unsuccessful psychotherapy, had discovered *est*. After assaulting me with the same ritual *est* phrases I had heard from countless other "graduates"—about having created the space in which to experience herself and about wanting to assist me in my understanding—she stated that in the three months since taking the training she had become "totally satisfied with her life." Although I firmly believed that *est* had been a positive experience for her, such complacency—aggravated by her not knowing at all *why* she was satisfied—did not bode well for the future. She seemed to be no more than the conduit—certainly not the source—of the statements she was making. Only when I mentioned specifically her apparent inability to speak spontaneously did any individuality return to her conversation.

This notion that psychological growth may be achieved through an act of will that takes into account neither one's own unconscious (behavior and activity) nor external social conditions is clearly embodied in the following advertisement from *Publishers Weekly* for Martin Shephard's *The Do-It-Yourself Psychotherapy Book*: "This book will save you thousands of dollars and give you control of your own life and your best self. *No More* Paid Advisors, Sex Hangups, Feeling of Inferiority, Psychosomatic Illness, Guilt. *Enjoy* More Personal Power, Boundless Sensual Pleasure, New-Found Self-Reliance, Your Birthright of Health, New Life-styles." It is a notion that leads to a narcissism perfectly expressed by an Esalen group leader named Shirley, in a conversation reported in the *Village Voice:*

"Leo," said Miriam, "you have to realize the important thing is living in the present moment. You have to be fully aware in the now, that's the trick."

"Beautiful," said Shirley, "beautiful. It's just like the Aquarian Age."

"Shirley," said Leo, "you've got to stop that Aquarian Age stuff. If this is the Aquarian Age, we're in trouble, we've been screwed by Nixon, we've been screwed by Ford, and we're letting Kissinger screw everyone he wants."

"I don't understand politics," said Shirley. "I don't know anything about politics, so I don't feel as if I'd been screwed. It's not part of my reality, so it's not true for me."

The current narcissism engendered by the idea of just "being oneself" involves the belief that psychological characteristics and sexual proclivities are entirely *conscious* choices made by the individual, and not functions of the unconscious or instinctual life as well. It is not uncommon these days to hear people speak about their homosexuality as a "preferred" form of sexual life or defend their three divorces on the grounds that "marriage simply doesn't work any more"—all as if what one is, what has become of one, has been nothing more than a *moral* choice, a decision to participate in a prevailing and attractive ideology; as if understand-

14

ing one's childhood experiences is irrelevant, just a quaint Freudian ploy to undermine one's will, one's ability to do and be exactly what one wants.

And, since to the psychobabbling mentality all behavior is a matter of taste, it also adopts in crude form the assertion (most widely publicized by R. D. Laing and Thomas Szasz) that there is no inherent difference between "sanity" and "insanity." Psychobabblers may concur that what differences there appear to be are determined by the presiding culture, but they show no interest in examining those relationships between culture and the individual.

The contemporary psychological air is scented with a secularized positive thinking, and, according to one former *est* trainer, "Life is nothing but one happy trail." Anything goes. What is, is, and what ain't, ain't, as the *est* punch line says. In fact, psychobabble describes anyone with a commitment or a highly developed interest as a *freak*. A composer is a music-freak, a writer a word-freak, a cyberneticist a computer-freak—as though one's profession were just one's chosen perversion or stimulant. "Do your own thing" goes beyond a mere libertarian attitude and dangerously implies an equality to all endeavors. Critical judgment succumbs to institutionalized tolerance. As social conditions degenerate, a tender but cruel optimism suffocates skepticism.[1] Confusion is not clarified, merely given the name "reality."

Psychobabble has quite naturally insinuated itself into many art forms, and in most cases this is no surprise. That we can now hear it regularly on television—that we even have a sitcom, *The Bob Newhart Show*, in which the lead character is a friendly psychotherapist—seems only fitting for a medium

[1] For an interesting discussion of the theoretical underpinnings of the human potential movement's ascendancy, one would do well to read Russell Jacoby's *Social Amnesia: A Critique of Conformist Psychology from Adler to Laing* (Beacon Press, 1975).

that reflects midcult values. In rock music the incidence of psychobabble is high, which is only natural for a form whose requirements of rhyme and accessibility limit the range of its insights.

Lines such as Todd Rundgren's "Get your trip together, be a real man" abound more than ever today, but some of the most eloquent psychobabble comes from John Denver, who, fresh from *est*, told a *Rolling Stone* interviewer in 1975:

> How far out it is to be a bird and fly around the trees. I am what I've always wanted to be and that is the truth. And I think—in fact, it's not what I think, but I observe that if people were to really take a good look at themselves, they are exactly the way that they have always wanted to be. . . . My experience is that if I can tell you the truth, just lay it out there, then I have totally opened up a space for you to be who you are and that it really opens up all the room in the world for us to do whatever we want to do in regard to each other. If I don't like you, I'll tell you. And that's great.

As for contemporary films that deal in psychobabble (*Easy Rider, Bob and Carol and Ted and Alice* and countless others), one is always tempted to praise highly those that capture the essence and cadence of psychobabble dialogue, simply on the basis of verisimilitude. But because film and rock music are always to some extent engaged in *representing* behavior, not scrutinizing it, they are easy targets to attack. One has to look elsewhere to find a medium that has truly suffered at the hands of psychobabble.

Such a victim is American publishing (although one might just as easily say it victimizes itself). Psychobabble's and publishing's influence on one another has been disastrous, and the number of psychobabble books offered to the public with a solemnity formerly reserved for great works is astounding.

Seventeen years ago, Alfred Kazin derided the Myth of Universal Creativity, which was engendered by the Freud craze in this country in the middle of the century—"The assumption," as he put it, "that every idle housewife was meant to be a painter and that every sexual deviant is really a poet." The time has never been more propitious than today for everybody and his or her therapist to spill the beans in print. To an older and still mistaken belief that one only has to be deemed neurotic in order to create has been added the more recent societal sanction—that, according to the spirit of the cult of candor, it is actually virtuous to reveal to as many people as possible the tragedies and erotic and emotional secrets of one's private life. It seems that all you need these days to qualify as a bona fide author is a few hours of therapy and a minimal ability to compose grammatical sentences.

This literary incontinence has affected even our serious writers, as Gore Vidal once pointed out in a review of John Dos Passos's *Midcentury*. He called it "a terrible garrulousness in most American writing, a legacy no doubt of the Old Frontier." He went on: "For every Scott Fitzgerald concerned with the precise word and the selection of relevant incident, there are a hundred American writers, many well regarded, who appear to believe that one word is just as good as another, and that anything which pops into the head is worth putting down. . . . Most of our writers tend to be recorders. They tell us what happened last summer, why the marriage went wrong, how they lost custody of the children, how much they drank and whom they laid. . . ."

Books written in the spirit of psychobabble share this quality of aimless chronicling, but with a light dusting of psychology. These books almost always seem, as the phrase goes, "touchingly human," but in their simplification of psychological issues they participate in what Herbert Marcuse has termed (referring to some of the neo-Freudians, to whom psychobabblers are indebted) "the laboring of the obvious, of everyday wisdom" and what Jacoby has called, after him, "the monotonous discovery of common sense." Books of psychobabble present revelation uninformed by history, unmediated by theory or understanding; they are, for all their professed drama, like verbal home movies.

In *Intimate Feedback: A Lover's Guide to Getting in Touch with Each Other* by Barrie and Charlotte Hopson (published in 1975 by Simon & Schuster) we are offered these insights:

> Who am I? This is a question which has always been central to man's awareness of himself.
>
> Human existence is exemplified by one person trying to communicate with others.
>
> When couples say that they have nothing new to learn about each other, this is due to stereotyped communication patterns, unless they really do not like one another and have no interest in their partner.

Other books, such as Harry C. Lyon, Jr.'s, *It's Me and I'm Here!* (Delacorte Press, 1974), are more personalized guides. Even the title suggests a giddy infatuation with self-actualization—and the contents do not disappoint. Lyon was raised comfortably middle-class, attended West Point, bedded numerous women to prove himself, and then realized that he was living by a morality that directed emotional traffic without getting him anywhere. Off to Esalen. In the book's foreword, human potential psychologist Carl Rogers tells us that he "became thoroughly convinced that [Lyon] was 'for real.'" Lyon concurs heartily in his own introduction:

> Look, my life has been exciting. It has been strange and painful, and I don't quite know what to make of it myself. But I want you to touch it—touch me—because

I so much want to reach you. I want you to feel that pain and joy I have felt.

One tendency of psychobabble is to interpret each new phase of life as "liberation," regardless of its context. Take Louise Diane Campanelli, whose recent book, *Sex and All You Can Eat* (Lyle Stuart, 1975), is a masterpiece of the banality of liberation. Repulsed by her husband's obesity, she went out and had, at last count, sixty-two lovers. Her psychiatrist has provided an introduction in which he tells us that the book's theme "concerns the poignant life story of a young woman of foreign parentage who is caught in a clash of culture, as well as in an identity crisis." Sounds like Henry James, but it reads like *True Confession* by an M.A. in sociology. She writes:

There is a tremendous amount of adultery going on in America today. Going on, indeed, at this very minute. Yes, while you read, thousands upon thousands of couples are coupling in hotel and motel rooms, in the rear seats of automobiles, and in "his" or "her" bedroom because the spouse is safely away.

Her book is sprinkled with routine references to childhood events, but mostly it reports on her numerous sexual encounters, including this comment on her career in fellatio: "You have to know what you're doing, and you have to know when to quit, but even a girl with a little mouth can go a long way."

The fact that women are reclaiming the emotional, professional and sexual prerogatives so long denied them has been the source of many excellent books, but it has also been the inspiration for volumes of psychobabble that reduce complex feminist arguments and impulses to the merely sexual. Promiscuity always makes good copy, and if it can be advertised in the context of more serious issues—whether it actually discusses these issues or not—it acquires, in addition, the patina of intellectual respectability. This is precisely what happens in *The Sexually Aggressive Woman* by psychotherapist Adelaide Bry (Peter Wyden, 1975). *The Sexually Aggressive Woman* is composed largely of transcribed interviews with women who responded to Bry's posted notices and personal want ads asking that women who considered themselves sexually aggressive come forward.

In accordance with the two-dimensionality of psychobabble, any thoughtful analysis must be avoided in favor of behavioral observation and an extolment of "liberation" in virtually any form. We never get an analysis from Bry of why sexually aggressive women are that way, only a description of *how* they are that way. No illuminating psychological theory is invoked; Bry settles for saying that "We do not know why one woman assumes power while another does not. . . . There are theories, of course, but the mystery still has not been solved to the satisfaction of most." There are theories, of course, but why waste precious time? If the mystery cannot be solved, let's just keep examining the evidence over and over. The evidence in *The Sexually Aggressive Woman* consists of five wives and mothers, eight single women between the ages of thirty-two and fifty, and seven young single women, all of whom chronicle their sex lives. At the end of each transcription, Bry appends her italicized commentaries which, in fact, are no more than blistering fusillades of paraphrase and cliché. Joan, for example, is thirty-two, divorced, a junior high school English teacher. She details her active sex life and then sums up her own character succinctly with the phrase, "I'm me." Bry's comment on Joan reads, in part: "She revels in being herself. She rejects male-defined standards of beauty. 'I'm me,' she says. I am woman, I am sexual, but I am also me. I conform to my own criteria."

One year later, Bry surfaced with another book called *est: 60 Hours That Transform Your Life* (Harper & Row, 1976). In it, through the description of her *est* volunteer work, one gains some insight into her further flight from critical thinking. "The high point of the weekend," she writes, "came when the man in charge of logistics said to me, after I had mapped the shortest and most efficient route to the bathrooms, 'Thank you, Adelaide. You have done an excellent job in writing these instructions.' Wow! I was high for hours. From which I *got* that it's a lot more satisfying to be *on purpose* than scattered, *and* that I enjoy someone else's approval for a job well done." How can one respond to such perception but to cheer Ms. Bry's recognition of the already apparent?

If women are testing their independence these days, and finally making their domestic jailbreaks, then many men are certainly suffering as a result. Male response has been in many quarters a sudden and useful self-scrutiny, sometimes culminating in pedantic apologies for being men in the first place (in America, where movements proliferate like fast-food outlets, the new femininity must be met with a new masculinity—all God's children gotta have instant ideology). In the case of the pseudonymous Albert Martin and his *One Man, Hurt* (Macmillan, 1975), though, one hears only a bewildered lament. In 1972, his wife of twenty years asked him for a divorce. He couldn't understand why she didn't love him any longer, but many readers of his 278-page account will no doubt get some idea. Martin, in reality a New York public relations executive by another name, has a very two-dimensional understanding of his failed marriage and yearns, in prolix paragraphs, for an uncluttered security in the face of this threat to his androcentric world-view, one he is not in the least capable of modifying to accommodate his wife's side of the story. One can certainly sympathize with

Martin's pain, but his book is essentially self-justification dressed as compassion—and reading it can only inspire respect for his ex-wife, who has not felt similarly compelled to burden the reading public with her grievances.

When Martin attempts to be reflective, he succeeds only in attributing a large portion of his troubles to external forces:

> I think there are bad times to be certain things in history. It was bad to be a witch in Salem in the 1700s, bad to be a Negro in America before May 1954 [and it's a ball being one now?], bad to be a polio victim the year before they discovered the vaccine. And I know it is bad to be in marital trouble in America today because the times have never been worse for getting effective help.

The implied equation of his predicament with religious persecution, racial prejudice, and physical handicap is an indication of his refusal to see the extent to which *he* is an accomplice to his own woe and not just the "hurt" victim of his title. Publication of *One Man, Hurt* is further proof that nowadays there is someone ready to hear anybody's complaint.

The publishing industry's enthusiasm for psychobabble of the preceding variety as well as of the more explicitly therapeutic strain (*How to Be Your Own Best Friend, How to Be Awake & Alive, When I Say No, I Feel Guilty*, etc., etc.) was perhaps foreshadowed during the past decade by the success of confessional books. To name but a very few, Gestalt therapy "refounder" Fritz Perls's *In and Out the Garbage Pail* was a lesson in incontinent narcissism ("I am becoming a public figure," he announces on page one); R. D. Laing's *Knots* made relationships seem irresistibly complex; Erica Jong aired her own fantasies in the fictional *Fear of Flying*; and Nigel Nicolson's tribute to his famous parents Harold

Nicolson and Vita Sackville-West, *Portrait of a Marriage*, endowed the polymorphous perverse with historical dignity: Sexual fantasies, helped along by James Joyce's love letters to his wife and Nancy Friday's *My Secret Garden* and *Forbidden Flowers*, seem to have achieved the status of art.

Now that the confessional genre has been appropriated by every other divorcee, adulterer, and successfully therapized individual, there is no end in sight to the number of truisms published as striking revelation, to the prurience parading as sociology. Is it that society has become so atomized that the emotional strength once derived from communities, the extended family, and the simple observation of life is now thought to be obtainable only from self-help books? The popularity of psychobabble has eclipsed the public taste for literature and psychological theory. Novelists are going out of business while small-town gurus appear on talk shows to exchange insights with Joey Bishop.

There is more self-help and psychological advice literature on the bookshelves right now than ever before—*Your Inner Conflicts—How to Solve Them; How to Give and Receive Advice; How to Live with Another Person; Free to Love: Creating and Sustaining Intimacy in Marriage; Stand Up, Speak Out, Talk Back; When I Don't Like Myself.*

Please! one wants to cry—no more books by unhappy housewives crying, "I've just got to be me!" No more female ad agency executives telling me how they make men want to get into their pants at singles bars! No more divorced men screaming for justice! No more daydreams of Great Danes with searching tongues! Enough!

In the chapters that follow, it should become clear that the word "psychobabble" does not refer simply to certain modes of expression, but to a social mood as well—a verbal anxiety, a certain sort of disposition to talk about oneself, a

23

way of thinking. Most of the elements described by psychobabble are neither new nor unique, but they seem to have forcefully converged in the seventies.

As a designation for popular jargon, the term "psychobabble" has to be used with some circumspection. It does not *necessarily* imply a shallowness of understanding. For example, honesty or being "up front" is generally a good policy, but it can also become a nervous habit or a subtle petition for someone else's confession to which one has no right. Being "open" is a worthy ambition, unless it comes to mean merely using one's vulnerability as a calling card. "Getting it together" may denote a very real effort at psychic integration with all the harrowing revelations that entails, but it may also mean no more than a temporary reshuffling of needs to suit the moment. Talk about "the whole person" and "feeling whole" may actually refer to the recovery of an aspect of one's character that was formerly repressed or uncultivated, but it can also serve as a shorthand for an ideal that one indulges precisely in order not to work out problems closer at hand.

Arguing against psychobabble is not an argument *for* more elegant expression. It is—and this point will be refined in what follows—an argument for a language that has better access to the paradoxes of emotional life and therefore a language that is more revealing, more powerful, more therapeutic. Here a warning is in order: this book does not culminate in a radical new proposal for how we all should talk, and those who expect one will be disappointed. Nor does this book take the term "psychobabble" so seriously that it proposes a counterpsychobabble; that is, a systematic vocabulary to use *against* psychobabble. Those games are left to others.

Finally, there are those who will claim that psychobabble is a positive cultural sign, for it shows that many people are becoming less fascinated with materialism (some to the point of repudiating the material world and its demands altogether) and more curious about their interior life and motives in general. As a man of my father's age told me recently, "When we were your age, we didn't think about being people." Now, "being people" obsesses us. But it must be remembered once again that there is a hitch in this freedom to contemplate our "total personalities"; that freedom, such as it is, has been won by some at the cost of the continuing fragmentation of personalities. And, as Herbert Marcuse pointed out over twenty years ago, those who have the freedom to be "people" have it only as a condition of what he calls "repressive desublimation," that, in Marcuse's words, "in a period when the omnipotent apparatus punishes real nonconformity with ridicule and defeat—in such a situation the neo-Freudian philosopher tells the individual to be himself and for himself."

This stage of therapeutic consciousness and introspection has its materialistic side as well. "Keeping up with the Joneses" has been transformed into a Wholer-than-Thou attitude. Insight, packaged as psychobabble, has, become a commodity. A conviction in the noble savagery of freely playing emotions and a return to the romantic transcendental notion that God and everything else noble is right there already, inside us, hammering at the door of consciousness— these ideas about what "liberation" is seem now to have displaced in the popular mind an understanding of the difficult, dialectical nature of growth.

Psychobabble is not merely the verbal rent we pay to contemporary American life in the seventies. Increasingly, it *is* that life.

DAVID VISCOTT:
Sensitivity, Inc.

DAVID VISCOTT is more than a psychiatrist turned successful author of self-help books. Viscott, just under forty, is a psychobabble cottage industry unto himself, *the* entrepreneur of sensitivity in the thinnest-skinned decade of the century, a whiz kid from Dorchester, Massachusetts, with a black bag of behavioral nostrums, a *macher* with a psychodynamic message.

"Don't feel guilty about becoming a winner," he says in one of his numerous books, *How to Make Winning Your Lifestyle*. "Humility," he personally informs me while navigating through a Boston suburb in his pot-roast-colored Mercedes, "is a lot of shit." He once joked to a newspaper reporter: "If tomorrow morning I woke up and they said, 'You're the President of the United States,' it would take me approximately an hour to settle in. That hour would be spent understanding how the phones on my desk work and who my aides are."

"Someone told me," he says, "that I was a *Lamed-Vovnik*." According to the Midrash, the traditional Jewish interpretation of scripture, there are in any generation thirty-six ordinary humble individuals through whom the world finds its moral guidance. Viscott figures he may just be one of them.

In any case, *this* he's sure of: "If I went to the West Coast and settled in any town, I'd have a cult within a week!"

Not all self-help writers may share Viscott's sense of well-being, but they certainly aren't suffering these days. The realm of self-help literature is to psychiatrists, psychotherapists, researchers, and the clergy what Hollywood once was to Fitzgerald, Faulkner, and Mann—a sunny climate where one could earn good money and exposure while the best of one's talents atrophied from lack of exercise. And in self-help literature, as in Hollywood, the posture can be maintained with some honor, for a large audience actually appears to benefit from one's efforts. Self-help has never been bigger business than in the seventies. Five of the top ten nonfiction bestsellers in 1975 were self-help books. New titles and new authors appear weekly, and the return on a writer's investment is often quite lucrative. One 1976 book, *Your Erroneous Zones*, written by psychotherapist Wayne W. Dyer in thirteen days, sold 150,000 copies in its first six months. "Mental health is not complex, involved or hard work," says Dyer. "It ought to be just common sense." The same goes for self-help books themselves.

The distinctions between most self-help volumes—whether mere doodlings of folk wisdom or sincere efforts to paraphrase serious ideas—are insufficient to justify their number. A critique of any one author's production holds surprisingly true for the genre these days. But the case of a figure as prolific and intriguing as David Viscott is perhaps more interesting than most.

For one thing, his story involves more than just self-help books. Back in the late sixties, Viscott, then a young psychiatrist with a Brookline practice aimed at creative and theatrical types, joined forces with Jonah Kalb, a journeyman writer and advertising executive, to form a company called Sensitivity Games, Inc. Together, they invented an immensely clever adult game called Sensitivity. In fact, says Viscott, they put together "the entire sensitivity movement." After creating the game, which evolves during its enactment into an encounter group situation for the participants, they developed Sensitivity Greeting Cards, the most successful line of greeting cards in the country in 1970 and still on the market.

"They're classics," Viscott says with customary reserve. He had observed friends playing Sensitivity and was encouraged by the way in which those not normally inclined to open up emotionally with others did so within the structure of the game. "I started to think about that. I was having a lot of difficulty in my relationship with my wife at the time. One of the ways I got through to her was by writing down a statement I wished to make. I thought, Jesus, if only people could express specific feelings the way they were asked to in the Sensitivity game. So I knocked off about two hundred fifty statements one weekend and came into the office on Monday and showed them to Jonah. He knocked the list down to the thirty best, rewrote them, and came up with the inkblot art concept. The inkblots were colorful, a useful lock-in with psychology, and an interesting visual display. We put them together, hopped a plane to California and sat down with the people at Buzza in Anaheim and blew them out of their seats. We had the hottest greeting card line in the country.

"Eventually, we kept a computerized index of what cards were selling where. In Houston, for instance, the largest selling card was a single red dot on the outside—when you opened it up it said, 'This is no better, and a lot lonelier.' There's a lot of divorce down there in Houston."

For the institutionalized banality of traditional American greeting cards—"You're the gosh darn best grandpappy a little feller could have!"—Viscott and Kalb substituted an institutionalized openness. Sincerity could now be obtained at the corner drugstore along with one's Valium. The cards said things like "Thank you for giving when I couldn't ask" and "I think you use being hurt as a weapon against me." Then there was a line of party glasses that also sported ink-blots with messages that brought intimacy to the cocktail hour, candor to the chip dip. One said, "Tell me something about yourself you've never told anyone else before"; another said, "Whom would you like to meet here? I'll go over and introduce you." "These," says Viscott, "were things that could alter the dynamics of a party. Then I had a thing called Emotional Blocks—you throw them and put them together in order and they say things like, "Make up a story about the person here least likely to believe in Santa Claus."

This last idea was never marketed, but Viscott and Kalb were already remarkably successful. When materialism had started to sour and American middle-class consciousness began to shift to psychotherapeutic activism, Viscott and Kalb were not caught napping. "We banked on that shift as long ago as 1968 and '69," Viscott recalls. "That's the mood we predicted and decided to ride on. I had a feeling the country was falling apart, that a lot of people were being pushed and we had built up a Xerox and an IBM and a GM culture that really didn't work. In business, I was meeting a lot of business's top personnel and I was meeting a lot of frightened people who didn't know how to interact. I had the feeling that there was a wave coming and it would start to drown a lot of people; they would be swimming for their lives. And I felt that there were a lot of things people needed to know that they weren't getting."

Viscott and Kalb already knew what others need to know, and they began distributing their wisdom with the help of marketing surveys and a public relations firm in New York. They learned how public opinion was formed and within one year sold twenty-five million Sensitivity Greeting Cards. "We saw the niche," Dr. Viscott says, "and we created our own leverage in that niche and everyone who came after us would have to follow."

If, about this time, a Los Angeles psychotherapist named Arthur Janov was shaping Primal Therapy, yet another of the exclusive cures for neurosis, a former door-to-door salesman named Jack Rosenberg was formulating a fascinating non-cure called *est* that within five years would claim 90,000 satisfied customers, and countless others were hammering out their solutions to widespread malaise, David Viscott was doing nothing less than helping to establish the whole national climate of insearching. He was seeding the clouds of candor in this country and when it began to rain, it would rain not only confessions throughout the land, but pennies from heaven for Viscott himself. Many of his self-help books have sold over 100,000 copies, and one, he says, has sold half a million in paperback and been published in several other countries.

Viscott's primary occupation these days is authoring self-help books. Sensitivity Games, Inc., after all, was really just business, but writing self-help literature is, well, it's not quite art, but it's not all business. "I've always had a literary flair," he says, "but it's never been able to come out in the self-help books." What does come out is at least well-meant, if not Goethe. As a psychiatrist trained in the Freudian style, his popular writing is rooted in depth psychology. His intent is not to moralize, but to show readers how the dynamics of human behavior work. He wanted to help people after he discovered around 1970 that he had his own "enormous sense of completeness."

Dwight Macdonald remarked in his 1954 essay "Howto-ism" that "Howto writers are to other writers as frogs are to mammals; their books are not born, they are spawned. A Howtoer with only three or four books to his credit is looked upon as sterile." By these standards, Viscott is almost fertile. He has, by the time you read this, published eight or nine books, five of them specifically self-help (and some of them discussed with Johnny Carson), and is currently pregnant with projects, both literary and other. As for the other, he now has nine different greeting card lines; he has completed the music and libretto for a musical based on his 1974 book *How to Live with Another Person* and also has a Broadway play in the works; he has appeared as resident psychiatrist on ABC's *Good Morning, America* show, is doing syndicated spots for the network and murmurs about someday co-hosting his own network talk show; he is cutting a comedy album in Minneapolis that features, among other psychiatric take-offs, impersonations of a German and an Indian doctor; he has vague plans to open, as an outgrowth of a forthcoming book called *Natural Therapy,* a series of walk-in psychological service centers for what he calls "normal people"; he lectures widely; he still tries to find time to work on a cancer research project begun in his medical school days; he is an accomplished musician.

Much of this psychotherapeutic peanut butter is perhaps spread rather thin on Viscott's career sandwich, but he is a man of infinite energy and many talents. His *real* ambition—well, at least one of them—is to become a literary writer and, in fact, some of his literary outpouring has done him modest justice. His 1972 best-selling *The Making of a Psychiatrist* (volume two of this book should appear soon) is an effectively drawn, anti-authoritarian account of his psychiatric residency at a Boston hospital. In it one not only learns a great deal about the nature of American psychiatry, but also gets a whiff of Viscott's dislike for the imperious reticence that seems to be psychoanalysis's legacy in this country (Freud himself was often quite voluble behind the couch and feared what would happen to psychoanalytic practice in America when it was given over entirely to medical school graduates).

Viscott was the "best resident" at the time at his hospital. "I saw that I was a therapeutic person and that I was a therapeutic person not because I was a psychiatrist, not because I was trained, which I was. I mean," Viscott addresses the analysts of America, "the psychoanalysts like to say to me now, 'Well, you haven't been through psychoanalysis yourself.' [Viscott had an aborted, unsuccessful psychoanalysis with a doctor so laconic that he made, as Helen Lawrenson has said of Fred Astaire, Gary Cooper sound like a magpie.] Well, fuck it, mister, I could sit behind a couch and do analysis and carry it off just as well as you. And better."

A year later, Viscott followed with *Dorchester Boy: Portrait of a Psychiatrist as a Very Young Man*. This at times lyrical chronicle of a Jewish boyhood doesn't rate with Isaac Rosenfeld's *Passage Toward Home*, for example, but it does reveal a moving, if sometimes facile, literary feel. Of his very first published book, a 1970 hospital novel called *Labyrinth of Silence*, Viscott says: "It didn't work but sections of it were hauntingly moving, they just blew you away."

His first self-help book, *Feel Free*, published in 1971, is a sort of late-hippie tract, a positivist exhortation to break away, particularly from confining and unhappy marriages, one of which Viscott was involved in at the time. The book is a critique of the scarcity mentality born of the Depression and the resulting middle-class culture, which sacrificed per-

sonal growth on the altar of financial security and technological fetishism. It is a vote, perhaps at times too ardently
cast, for the pleasure principle. If you want to flee a bad
marriage, or resign as a businessman to pursue painting full-
time, says Viscott, do it; only you can make the decision
since neither friends nor a society that thrives on the repression of the individual can be expected to lend support. There
are some valuable passages here, particularly Viscott's examples of the best way to broach the subject of major
changes with family and friends.

His second self-help book, *How to Make Winning Your
Lifestyle,* antedated by three years the best-selling guides to
success of 1975, Robert J. Ringer's *Winning Through In-
timidation* and Michael Korda's *Power! How to Get It, How
to Use It* (interestingly, Korda is Viscott's latest editor).
Here, again, Viscott rooted out the coming social trend. As
American institutions grow more bureaucratic and deperson-
alized, and individuals more alone, the belief in the virtues of
active personal manipulation materializes. If people cannot
overcome or change institutions, then at least they can appropriate corporate styles of conduct and repossess the illusion of autonomy. As one Harvard business psychologist said
in *Time* magazine of Ringer's and Korda's works: "The
books give permission to attack. They legitimize the underlying aggression in people." The books isolate power and in-
timidation from their origins in a particular economic system
and then proffer them to readers as the only remnants of
integrity left in a world that has beaten them down.

Viscott's *Winning* shares with its descendants that pecu-
liarly American optimism and its corollary anti-intellectual-
ism: "How much brains do you think it takes to be successful? It's not brains that determine success," Viscott writes.
"There are professors on skid row and a lot of geniuses who
can't get ahead. So it can't be brains alone that guarantee

success." There is also the same attention to the details of superiority. Korda has his "power gaze"; three years earlier, Viscott counseled in "Ten Rules for Acting with Authority": "Do not look people in the eye when you speak with them, but look at the middle of their forehead, one-half inch above their eyebrows. This makes it difficult for them to cause you to change your facial expression which is often the first sign that you are backing down. Have a prepared ending ready to cut off conversations."

Viscott, unlike some others, does not confine his message—"Learn to cope with that selfishness and not feel guilty about it"—to a business context; he offers some good, practical advice on how to listen, how to wait, how to look at both sides of an issue, as well as a sound two-page chapter called "Everything You Always Wanted to Know About Winning at Sex."

Having thus helped his audience to feel free and develop a winning lifestyle, in 1974 Viscott published *How to Live with Another Person*. Despite the fact that this book purports to concern itself with relationships between lovers and spouses, one gets the feeling, having read it, that its contents are virtually the same as his previous two self-help books. This is a remarkable thing about American self-help books in general—each seems to be the same roll of Life Savers, only with the colors arranged in a different order. In *How to Live*, one is treated to already familiar exclamatory refrains—"Every person has a right to be himself, the person he is" and "You have a right to become the person you were destined to become" and an endless succession of aphorisms about the healing properties of love and respect. "Without love, nothing is right. A life without love is not right. A life without love is a world without love." Then: "We ought to love each other for what we are and for our potential for becoming."

In *The Making of a Psychiatirst*, Viscott complained that

34

the use of psychiatric jargon turned him off. But when I, in turn, complained to him about his use of this psychobabble, he seemed oblivious to its recurrence throughout his texts, confirming one's suspicion that people tend to see only highly technical or complex jargon as obfuscatory, while conceptually primitive nonsense is somehow perceived as democratic and enlightening. Although assembled on a foundation of psychoanalytic insight, *How to Live* and, two years later, *The Language of Feelings* are fabricated from phrases often deafening in their simplicity. Who would take exception to this line from *How to Live:* "Conflict is the language of anger?" One could, in fact, reverse some of the words so that it read "Anger is the language of conflict" and still be disinclined to take issue. "Anger," it might even be said, "is the conflict of language."

"You are your feelings and thoughts, your actions and intentions," Viscott writes. "You have a right to feel whatever you feel, to be whoever you are." This sounds almost like a man talking in his sleep. If you *are* those four things, why would you then need a *right* to be them? And if you *do* need a right, what is the ethical content or the context of that right? Other questions elbow in: just because you *have* a feeling or a thought or are the agent of an action, does that mean you *are* that feeling or thought or action? And aren't you also the result of other people's actions, intentions, thoughts, and feelings? Aren't you also the past? But let's not overdo it; the point is simply that numerous philosophical and psychological confusions are inevitably lodged in psychobabble like this.

Although Viscott's first two self-help books had a certain edge to them, a usefulness for the discriminating reader, in *How to Live with Another Person* he only disentangles the issue of human relationships from its dense web of social, political, and economic considerations and then isolates that

35

issue in a small bed of cotton: "To live with another person is . . . to give up your illusions through love"; "Love is always now. . . . An old love never dies, it just exists in a quieter place." Viscott lubricates this sermon on togetherness with short, italicized poems, such as: "But let's not hate each other for what we're not/The day's too pretty and we could love again." If, as Viscott claims, he wrote *How to* in three weeks one would probably need a fine Swiss stopwatch to time the composition of his poems.

"What I'm saying," Viscott says, "is no one has ever come out with this stuff so clearly or simply that a fucking truck driver can pick this book up and say, 'Aha! When I'm angry, it's because someone has hurt my feelings!'" This claim to originality is as comical as its elitism is disquieting. Does he think that it is truck drivers and not academics, for instance, who stand to benefit most from common wisdom? And it is not entirely clear why anyone at all needs a book to make so simple a connection between anger and hurt. But Viscott—and a long tradition of self-help literature writers—evidently trusts the public's insatiable need to be reminded of the obvious.

Reminding others of the Already Obvious is a difficult task, for no one likes to be tutored in what he already knows. Therefore, the person presenting the Already Obvious must be careful to present it as the Familiar Revelation. Viscott says of one of his books, *The Language of Feelings*, that it "was written to link together the intellectual with the feeling by taking some short cuts and it does that, but"—and here Viscott, as he often does, seems to capitalize his speech—"I'M NOT SURE HOW, BUT I THINK IT DOES IT THROUGH ITS *PRISTINE CLARITY*. I mean, what look like redundancies and repetitions are not. Each time something is repeated, it's repeated at a different level of truth." This is a good example of how someone presents the Already Obvious.

Perhaps what Viscott sees in the following is an example of repetition at a different level of truth; if so, truth must in his mind be constructed somewhat like a high-rise municipal parking lot in which every level looks like every other, particularly when you're trying to find your car. In *Feel Free*, his first self-help effort, Viscott offered a psychodynamic scheme that, as far as it goes, is good basic psychoanalytic theory:

> When a person suffers a real or imagined loss he feels hurt. Because something has been taken away, he feels empty or worthless. As a result, he becomes angry at the person he believes hurt him. If his anger is not resolved or allowed to be expressed, it will grow and lead to feelings of guilt. Guilt is anger that has turned inward. If unchecked, it may lead to feelings of depression. Anxiety is the fear of the loss in the first place. This also may be real or imagined.

Five years later, this thought reappears in *The Language of Feelings* as a passage of which Viscott is particularly proud, as if he had just invented it. It is printed in upper-case letters:

ANXIETY IS THE FEAR OF HURT OR LOSS.
HURT OR LOSS LEADS TO ANGER.
ANGER HELD IN LEADS TO GUILT.
GUILT, UNRELIEVED, LEADS TO DEPRESSION.

In a chapter of *The Language of Feelings* entitled "Hurt and Loss," Viscott's penchant for repetition is polished to a fine skill. In the space of six pages, he expresses the same thought—that people must confront their own vulnerability in order to do something about it—in a variety of ways:

Accepting vulnerability instead of trying to hide it is the best way of adapting to reality. (p. 35)

The major turning point for most people is to accept their insecurity and to stop trying to hide it. (p. 37)

It's a bright day when a person can understand that his imperfections are only human and that trying to conceal problems only makes them more obvious to others and even more difficult to correct. (p. 38)

You can't learn to grow from an experience you deny, including the experience of being hurt. (p. 38)

. . . you can profit a great deal from your experience of being hurt—see and understand yourself, including your shortcomings . . . (p. 38)

If you want to grow, begin by accepting the fact that like everyone else you are human, vulnerable, and subject to hurt—out of it can come your best chance for a liberating piece of the truth. (p. 40)

Viscott may indeed have a short memory for his own statements, or else he may simply feel that there is a delicate art in reiteration. In psychotherapy, insights and interpretations need to be pronounced over and over again because a patient tends to isolate insight intellectually unless he is reminded of it in connection with his actual behavior and his recollections of the past; but in a book, which is not psychotherapy, such repetitions serve only as a warm bath of advice for readers to languish in.

Viscott's self-quotation is also evident in the openings of his books. *Feel Free* begins: "The chances are, if you're really honest with yourself, that you won't do it this year either. You'll stay in the same situation, in the same role, in spite of how much you hate it." His second self-help book, *How to Make Winning Your Lifestyle*, begins: "It's painful to admit, but unless something drastic happens to you, you probably won't find yourself in the winner's circle this year either. You'll keep on making the same old mistakes and miss your best opportunities while others capitalize on theirs." "Come on, admit it," *How to Live with Another Person* starts. "You've been living with someone for a while now and you sometimes think you've made a mistake, a big mistake."

Viscott's tendency to oversimplify blossoms in *The Language of Feelings*. Here his intention is to write an intelligent reduction of psychodynamic theory for those who suffer from what during the last part of the nineteenth century was popularly called "neurasthenia." "My object," Viscott tells me, "is to reach not the real sick people, but the housewife in Des Moines who once went to see a psychiatrist who gave her some pills, and she didn't get better, she's still nervous, so a friend tells her to read *The Language of Feelings* and she begins to understand what's wrong with her life. You should see the boxes of fan letters I get from people I've helped!"

To some degree he succeeds in making plain obscurely worded theories. What the lady in Des Moines gets is basic psychological advice, obtainable from a million other sources —including Viscott's other books—that it's important to face one's feelings because they won't go away by themselves. But it is all dressed up in a way that raises one's hopes for easy solutions (were it not so attired, of course, Viscott's message would prove far less profitable for him).

Viscott isolates the notion of "feelings" as a discrete field of behavior quite divorced from the intellect. He must know better, know that feelings have meaning because they are conceptualized, because they are digested through one's system of seeing the world, because, also, feelings are often assigned meaning and value by specific cultural conditions. Yet he writes about them as if the key to well-being were simply a question of coaxing feelings out of their hiding places in the psyche so that they can be tamed in short order.

At times, Viscott demonstrates that indeed he is not completely taken in by his own psychobabble; he cautions, for instance, that purely cathartic devices like screaming or pillow-pounding "can become ends in themselves," as they often do in scream therapies. But then he sidesteps neatly and proclaims that "feelings, in fact, *are* the world we live in." Furthermore, he writes, "Feelings are the truth." And then: "What is that self? Who are you? You are the person experiencing your feelings, creating your world."

Now that the issue has been defined as "feelings," Viscott, all the while making perfectly sensible points about hurt, loss, anxiety, guilt, anger, and depression, begins to drop hints about how to deal with disruptive feelings. But that project of working-though, which, in psychotherapy or through living itself, may take years, is here insinuated as something one just does. "Even though it seems impossible at times, the best way to manage anxiety is to avoid unnecessarily threatening situations and to begin to make yourself the most complete and strongest person you can be." After telling his readers how crucial it is to face one's feelings and, presumably, the situations that stir them, Viscott pirouettes and says they should *avoid* them! "Once a person has overcome his own dependency problems he becomes free to give, to support, to encourage and sustain." Clearly easier said than done, this is rather like telling someone that once he's made a million dollars, he'll be rich.

This kind of thinking produces honest, benign sentiments emptied of their depressing content—that overcoming dependency is truly a project one can never complete, but only come closer and closer to completing; that the only way to overcome anxiety is to begin to put your nose in it. In Joan Didion's fine essay, "On Self-Respect," she writes, "There is a common superstition that 'self-respect' is a kind of charm against snakes, something that keeps those who have it locked in some unblighted Eden, out of strange beds, ambivalent conversations, and trouble in general. It does not at all. It has nothing to do with the face of things, but concerns instead a separate peace, a private reconciliation." Although Viscott himself might join Didion in this definition, his books convey the sense that self-respect—or, in his phraseology, being the person you were meant to be—has everything to do with the surface of things, with decals of self-appreciation and enlightenment.

In Viscott's books there is no serviceable pessimism, no irony. Once, in Paris, I had grown very depressed and a self-possessed Moroccan in his early thirties who claimed to be a Scottish prince spotted me in a cafe as someone with a great deal on his mind. An M.D. with a psychospiritual bent, he promptly divined the source of my anxiety and I, impressed by his insights, attached myself to him for the day, or it might have been vice versa, it was hard to tell. Protected by his compassion, I allowed myself to sink lower into self-pity. Toward evening I was full of despair and, at one point, blurted hopefully, thinking that the prince would rescue me, "But tell me, things get better as you grow older, don't they?" The prince, who all day had addressed me with ironic respect as "sir," shook his head slowly and replied with a comforting brutality: "My dear sir, of course not. They get much worse!"

This tension is lost in Viscott's books where, one is told, "You don't need to create this person because you already *are* this person." Jung speaks of the process of individuation, by which he meant basically integration of the self, as one in

41

which "the individual becomes what he always was." Jung's notion at least implies the irony and pity of life spent in the acquisition of what one already possesses; the truth one finally arrives at may seem obvious, even redundant, but the process of arriving at it is nonetheless an arduous one of becoming. Viscott's message, on the other hand, appears to be that the whole, feeling person is already there, fully formed, if one only knew in what pocket to look.

With his self-help books, Viscott locates himself in an American mind cure and self-help tradition more than a century old. In the middle of the nineteenth century, those movements that took it as their goal to enable people to enlarge their lives and find peace of mind were concerned almost exclusively with the therapeutic benefits of religious faith. The message, as delivered by P. P. Quimby and his disciple Mary Baker Eddy, founder of Christian Science, was that to "think God's thoughts" was the cure for nervousness, neurasthenia, and confusion. Mind cure was a term that meant not intellectual solutions but a spiritual self-discovery, for God *was* Mind. The "cure" was not the result of an examination of one's past or the scrutiny of one's motives, as it was later to mean in Freudian psychotherapy, but rather the cure was faith, the cure was a result of "divine influx." The implication was that one got better because one *believed*, regardless of what it was that one believed in.

Beginning with William James, the idea of a subconscious was introduced to American mind cure. The idea that one's discontent had its origins in the self and in repressed ideas was a threat to the Protestant mind cure evangel. Could religion then be reduced to a psychology that excluded God? Well, not yet at least. James saw the subconscious as a conduit for divine thought and inspiration; it still had magical, mystical powers and was benign. If you wanted something bad enough, God would give it to you, but it now came to you through the subconscious. This was a curious compromise between theology and psychology; it still suggested that man could control his life by sheer will. It was a more enlightened belief than that of Mary Baker Eddy, who never got around to acknowledging the existence of a subconscious, but it still did not ask men and women to reckon with their own buried unpleasant feelings.

This theological perspective has survived to the present in, among others, Norman Vincent Peale, whose version of mind cure has been described by historian Donald Meyer as "a technique whereby a precarious ego represses recognition of its own precariousness."[1] Aspects of the current human potential movement share this repression of unruly unconscious elements.

However, as Freudian psychology and the birth of psychosomatic medicine made their impact in America during the early part of this century, mind cure began to lose its status as a religion and took on a more secular, scientific coloring as psychotherapy. Pastoral counseling—the dispensing of psychotherapy by clergymen—grew radically by the 1940s, symbolizing a rapprochement of faith and Freud.

Self-help books which played down the rigid, repressed, conscience-stricken character of organized religions while educating the public in Freudian psychological principles began to flourish. One of the many popular ones, *On Being a Real Person*, published in 1943 by a liberal Protestant minister named Harry Emerson Fosdick (who was the author of countless inspirational volumes), was a sophisticated layman's guide to therapeutic psychology. Fosdick sought to give his term "real person" a definite meaning: it meant

[1] I am indebted to Meyer's book, *The Positive Thinkers: A Study of the American Quest for Health, Wealth and Personal Power from Mary Baker Eddy to Norman Vincent Peale* (Doubleday, 1965), for this brief history and recommend it highly to those interested in the subject.

43

DAVID VISCOTT

someone who was fully integrated psychically. Integration,
after all, and Fosdick made this clear, had begun to supplant
religious salvation as a prevailing cultural ideal. Fosdick explained, through cautionary case studies as well as description, that becoming a "real person" did not suggest the perfection of self or the total removal of conflict, but rather the
achievement of a personal balance—in Fosdick's felicitous
phrase, "Integration is an affair of psychological government,
with all the recurrent dissents, tensions, and revolts to which
government, however united and strong, is subject." In considering the problems of self-acceptance and how to handle
anxiety and fear, he elucidated Freudian principles such as
sublimation, displacement, and projection. In doing so he
captured a sense of the psyche's complexity and of a *continuing* struggle to become "real." Fosdick was less interested in
glib reassurances than in truth: "Therapy," he wrote, "directed merely toward a happy adjustment to life is by itself
alone superficial." "Being a real person," which thirty years
thence would reappear in common speech as a somewhat
vague category of behavior, had in Fosdick a more precise,
psychoanalytic connotation.

In another best-selling book from the forties, *Peace of
Mind*, by a Boston rabbi by the name of Joshua Loth Liebman, one discerns the same effort to confront the tyrannical
aspects of religion and urge a liberation from false con-
science. Despite its evangelical title, Rabbi Liebman's book,
which went through thirty printings in paperback, was extremely Freudian in content. For instance, Liebman in one
chapter relates the concept of "love thyself" to the psychoanalytic ideas of healthy and unhealthy narcissism, and in
another compares the concept of "love thy neighbor" to the
psychological mechanisms of identification and ambivalence.
In parts an unabashedly ardent advertisement for Freudianism, *Peace of Mind* emphasized that repression, alas, "simply

44

has not worked" and encouraged readers not to be afraid of their feelings.

Thirty years later, David Viscott reheats the good old Freudian advice of the forties and serves it up as a new commentary on the human condition. The message is still edible and the public appetite has not slackened, but some of the texture and flavor has been lost. Fosdick, Liebman, Smiley Blanton and other self-help figures of the forties and fifties acknowledged their debts to Freud and his rather grim view of human endeavor. Liebman, for example, was able to speak of "the universal brotherhood of anxiety which binds the whole human race together." Viscott, however, glazes his therapeutic message with sweet admonitions to be the best "you" you can be. Sadly, he sees this as innovative. For the belief in religious faith that fills out Fosdick's and Liebman's prescription Viscott substitutes a faith in self that has no critical edge; once you free yourself, Viscott writes, "life becomes uncomplicated."

What is more, Viscott doesn't easily acknowledge his influences. He admits to having read five books in the last eight years, none of them in psychology. "I find," he says, "that in reading other people I forfeit my originality," when it would be closer to the truth to say that in not reading others, he forfeits the chance to appreciate his own lack of it.

"What I'm saying," he is saying, "is that I'm pretty much David."

"What do you mean by that?" I ask. "That you're you, you're yourself?"

"No, it means I'm pretty much uninfluenced."

"Is that good?"

"It works. If you could read a book that made you as successful at what you did as I am at what I do, you'd read it. And if knowing that not reading a book would make you that successful, you wouldn't read it." He giggles.

45

"But you don't know what you have to gain from reading other books sometimes until you've read them," I argue. "You've been exposed to so little."

"But I don't *wanna* read them," he complains, his voice now a good imitation of Jerry Lewis in *The Disorderly Orderly*. "I have too many things to write and when I'm finished with what I have to say, then I'll read."

"You might be surprised at how similar your books are to many others."

"*I noticed this!*" he says suddenly. "I pick up books in the stores once in a while. They *do* sound the same, it's true. But there's a difference. Their books are written. Mine . . . are *experienced*."

Viscott is now "experiencing" a book called *Risking*, which, in his words, is "a reorganization of how the life cycle operates." I ask whether this will be a revision of Erik Erikson's work on the subject.

"Never read Erikson," he replies.

But whether he has any historical perspective or not, Viscott undoubtedly helps many people. "Look," he beams, "I'm a psychiatrist. I'm well-trained, I'm even very good at it and, as a therapist, I'm just one of the best, I mean I really am. If you go into therapy with David, and I do it informally all the time, I mean a friend will drop by whom I haven't seen in two years who's been in therapy with someone and he'll sit down with me and he'll walk out half an hour later, saying 'I don't believe where I am, I've been trying to get to this point in therapy and my analyst always takes this detour, you know?' " The possibility that an analyst might take "a detour" in order to lead a patient from a modest confession that costs him nothing to a more significant disclosure that might stir up some anxiety but produce a deeper insight does not, apparently, interest Viscott.

"One woman who read *The Language of Feelings*," he

says, "had a problem with a rigid controlling mother and an ulcer and a grinding inside her chest for twenty years. She kept a bottle of Mylanta in her purse. Through reading the book she came to a revelation that allowed her to see through the problem with her mother and was able to give up a lot of expectations about her and lost the gnawing sensation and the indigestion." Reading a book may alleviate ulcers, but only for a time; put meddling mothers at a distance, but only momentarily. Chances are that the woman has not heard the last from her dyspepsia. What we see reflected in Viscott's success is the culture's impatience to get well, and fast.

Viscott lost patience with psychoanalysts years ago. "I know analysts," he says, voice escalating, "who went through the whole thing, the whole training, and they're REALLY SCHMUCKS!! And you can't be a good therapist if YOU'RE A SCHMUCK, EVEN IF YOU SAY THE RIGHT THINGS!!! I broke away because I found out that for shrinks the method became more important than the person, that the disease became more important than the patient. Something happened to psychiatry in America, where an obsessive-compulsive group had taken over the academic realm, a mercenary bunch had taken over the electroshock realm, and a lot of neuropsychiatry with medicine had taken over the other quarter, and then there was a bunch of hard-working therapists out there working their asses off, 50 percent of whom were competent, leaving 25 percent of psychiatry to be effective, but not all the time, and not with everyone. They say, 'Yes, I'll take this depressed old lady,' when they shouldn't take her because they can't handle her, or they'll say, 'Yes, I'll take this manic seventeen-year-old girl,' and end up putting controls on her instead of understanding her wish to run away from her dying father. What I found out was that there was more dishonesty, more hiding among psychiatrists than in any other profession I've seen because they had a rationalization for acting the way they wanted to be."

Viscott, of course, has his points. But one wonders how much personal concern he can have for the anonymous buyers of his books or for his millions of Sensitivity Card customers. And in turning so frantically from psychiatry to a production of self-help books, Viscott reminds one of a violin maker now interested only in carving kazoos—he's still making musical instruments, but one can't play very difficult tunes on them. The reduction of psychoanalytic theory to a chorus of aphorisms, however true, threatens to turn the riddles of human experience into one-liners and relegate Freud to second billing on a vaudeville marquee with Henny Youngman.

Certainly, Viscott's sanguineness is refreshing to many in an era of attenuated hopes. Personally, he is a pleasant individual to be around. He was "always the class clown" in school and confesses to his own "need for validation," but the effects of his attention-getting are greatly mitigated by humor and candor. Still, one gets the impression that in his manic self-confidence something important has eluded him—that he has found the ballpark, but missed the ballgame. Perhaps Viscott reveals that he shares this suspicion as well when he says, "So I'm writing the Psychology of Common Sense and, at forty-five, maybe there I'll be with no way to apply it, and I'll have to move on to something else."

But the self-assurance always returns: "I've always known I was special. I'm different and the difference will show in ten years. The other books will be gone and mine will still be on the shelf."

Now that is the statement of a man riding a wave of therapeutic optimism, and thinking all the while that he's just watching safely from the beach.

est:
The Self Is Fun to the Self

Dr. David Viscott and an army of self-help authors reinvented an upbeat mass psychology using scraps of psychoanalysis, religion and common sense; Werner Erhard went further. Understanding that books could do only so much in times of crisis, Erhard breathed life into the promises of well-being by hiking up the price of enlightenment from $8.95 hard cover to $250 and then $300 (insuring that the enlightenment offered would be taken just that much more seriously) and presenting an experience for which there was no merely literary substitute. Erhard made the word flesh, and the people came to listen.

The presence of Erhard Seminars Training is undeniable. *Est* has by now claimed over 90,000 graduates, among them corporate executives, politicians, actors, educators, and members of the mental health profession. The vast majority of graduates report a renewed ability to "experience" their lives, having gotten "It" during the two-weekend training now offered in a dozen American cities. In some respects, the benefits are quite palpable. Increased employability for one thing—many businesses say they "prefer" *est* graduates in their job ads. The affinity between *est* and American business is not incidental; one of *est*'s effects is to increase, via a detour through exercises in spiritual enlightenment, one's acceptance of the status quo. *Est* graduates are obedient and industrious. The organization's president is Don Cox, former General Manager of the Coca-Cola Bottling Company of California, and *est* itself is a formidable top-down corporate structure with its own highly protective public relations agency and public information office, a projected monthly gross of one million dollars, and numerous tax shelters. It runs special programs for blacks, prisoners, and children. It aspires to infiltrate the world with its spirit.

At one *est* function a year ago, a man stood up in the audience and addressed Werner Erhard, the man who started it all. "I'm a fifty-three-year-old psychiatrist," he said nervously, "and, listening to you, I've begun to think I should give up my practice. What do you suggest I do?"

Werner Erhard gave the psychiatrist an elliptical and finally patronizing answer. Then he went on to the next question from the audience. But I kept thinking about the fifty-three-year-old psychiatrist. A middle-aged mental health professional, some of whose patients might well have been in that very sea of people out of which he had momentarily risen, had publicly, in a downtown ballroom, doubted his own presumably lengthy career and asked the advice of a man he had never spoken to personally! What strange, arcane powers did this Werner Erhard possess that not only total strangers, but fifty-three-year-old shrinks, would lay their most fragrant insecurities at his feet like bouquets of flowers? The man on stage was obviously no guru off the last train from Bombay but a more indigenous doctor of the soul. Werner Erhard was ministering to a uniquely American historical spasm, some national epilepsy, some widespread inability to control one's life. To any of the psychiatrist's patients who might have been in the ballroom, it must have been scary—that the man in whose hands they had put their psychological growth, and at no small cost, was *himself* at the brink of existential collapse and had to ask Werner Erhard what to do!

Forty-year-old Werner Hans Erhard grew up in Philadelphia, where he was known as John Paul Rosenberg, Jewish by birth but a convert to the Episcopal Church. He sold cars in the 1950s, but even then, according to Bill Thaw,[1] his friend from that era, Rosenberg was interested in a more grandiose future, a master plan. In 1960, he left his first wife and four children and changed his name to Werner Erhard after reading an article in *Esquire* called "The Men Who Made the New Germany." By the late sixties, he was remarried, now had seven children in all, and was vice-president of *Parents' Magazine*'s Cultural Institute, which sold encyclopedias. From there, he passed on to the Grolier Society, which also sold books door-to-door, brushed shoulders with Scientology (which greatly influenced *est*), and evolved into a highly successful instructor of Mind Dynamics, a spiritual discipline started by Englishman Alexander Everett. By 1971, the itch for autonomy had grown irresistible. Erhard looked in his hands and found there an amalgam of Dale Carnegie, Scientology, Zen, the Protestant ethic, Taoism, door-to-door smarm, chutzpah, psychoanalysis, and certain oily arts of the

[1] For an interesting account of Erhard and *est*, see "The Fuhrer Over *est*" by Jesse Kornbluth, *New Times*, March 19, 1976, pp. 36–52.

American marketplace which, when warmed in his palms, metamorphosed into the gold of Erhard Seminars Training.

The suspicion is that John Paul Rosenberg knows something you don't.

And he does. First, he knows that if you put two hundred and fifty well-fed people in a room for as long as sixteen hours a day for four days spread out over two weekends, and if you take away their cigarettes, alcohol, reading material and other diversions, and if you give them only a couple of bathroom breaks, and, finally, if you've already pocketed their $300, then you have their attention. But second, and far more important, he and his other trainers know what to talk about while the nicotine hungers sharpen and bladders burn.

Werner Erhard knows about experience. He doesn't believe that talking about experience, that reading, thinking, or writing about it, is very useful; no, having the experience, experience itself, is the real payoff. Erhard had his big "catalytic" experience in 1971 when, parked in his wife's Mustang on the West Coast, he "got It"—that "what is, is" and "what ain't, ain't." He didn't spend any time in college or graduate school reading Freud, Lao-tzu, Kant, Sartre, Wittgenstein, Beckett, Wallace Stevens, Kierkegaard, or anybody else, but their thoughts speak through him (as do the thoughts of the less fashionable Dale Carnegie, Mary Baker Eddy, and Billy Graham). While others huddled in their library carrels Hi-Liting great thoughts with yellow felt-tip pens, Erhard was out selling. "I guess I was looking for Truth," he told one journalist, "but I was also using each technique in my business. I was lucky, because business only cares about results. In a university, I would have been crossing departmental lines and getting everybody mad, in a seminary I would have been burned as a witch, but business only cares about results."

He's getting results. Ninety thousand or so people can't be wrong. And they aren't. They're only about half wrong.

On a cold January evening in Boston, 2,612 people fill the seats of Symphony Hall to hear Erhard lecture. He is here to drum up some business for his anti-doctrine. "Drop the idea that there is any external pressure for you to take *est*," he says. "We couldn't care less if you took it or not. There is absolutely no difference—I repeat there is no difference—between those who have taken *est* and those who haven't, so drop any idea you have that . . ."

Everyone in the lobby wearing the official *est* badges signifying that they are now *est* volunteers is smiling, and one young woman in particular is sitting very erect in a folding chair looking as though, having swallowed 45 percent of the maximum dose of Thorazine while grinning, she had been rendered incapable of changing the expression on her face. The atmosphere is like coffee into which someone has emptied six packets of Sweet-'N'-Lo while you weren't looking. There's a lot of compulsive hand touching, gentle squeezes, tactile compliments.

On the way to my seat, a stately woman, an *est* graduate, intercepts me and says, "Frank! Frank!" I insist that I'm not and she finally agrees; she only *thought* I was the guy who lived with Amy. We fall into an amiable conversation during which she tells me that *est* made it possible for her to move out of the city to Newburyport and facilitated her divorce. (It is common to hear that *est* graduates have completed unfinished business—getting divorces, cleaning the bathroom, quitting bad jobs.) But she's in no mood to proselytize, which is fine with me, and I move on just in time to hear one man say to another: "You haven't done the training? You could use it, Jake."

I sit down next to a friend who's removed the name tag everyone is asked to wear upon entering. He thinks it's dehumanizing to wear name tags; there's an anonymity to identity so easily achieved. Two middle-aged couples in the row behind us seem themselves to be experiencing a form of depersonalization, perhaps just a mild sense of victimization, which they are working off by discussing Pet Rocks, a then new product—just a rock in a nice box—which is selling like hotcakes (the proceedings have already put me in an entrepreneurial mood, and I wonder why someone doesn't sell hermetically sealed hotcakes in nice boxes). I swivel and ask the couples whether they think *est* is just another Pet Rock and one of the women nods her head and then the man next to her says that Rosenberg is like Norman Vincent Peale, whom he heard many years ago, and where will he be in ten years? "I don't know," the woman replies. "Does it matter?"

Does it matter? Now, that is precisely the sort of comment that Werner Erhard would chew up and spit out. Does it matter? It doesn't matter at all—and it doesn't *not* matter at all. It just *is*.

Erhard strides on stage as the last notes of the *est* anthem, written by graduate John Denver, wind down on the tape. Erhard is tall, good-looking, with short dark hair barely over his ears. He is dressed in the approved *est* fashion, which he himself developed along with *est*'s wardrobe consultant Ron Mann (*est* officials and trainers are given a $1,500 clothing allowance): solid-color shirts open at the neck, flared slacks, sport coats. Erhard is youthful and gangly, moving rather like the guy who didn't make his high school basketball team and went out for public speaking instead. Inside his brown trousers, his legs appear as slender as Flexi-Straws. But there is self-assurance and a sense of possibility in his movements. The stage is very much his territory and were he suddenly to cartwheel or break into "Let's Spend the Night Together," one wouldn't be surprised.

But he doesn't. Instead he says, "I love you and I'm glad

54

to be able to participate in your lives." This is all very nice, but there is something slightly wooden about the delivery. First series of blandishments over, Erhard puts the audience through a process, one of the mental exercises that can go on endlessly in the actual training. The process is an experience, which means that the audience doesn't have to do anything but follow directions. No thinking about it is necessary, although some thinking can't be helped, and, like a good Transcendental Meditation instructor, he advises everyone just to let the thoughts come, don't fight them, but don't pay any attention to them either.

"Don't relax," he says. "People get tense when they relax."

The audience warms itself with some laughter. Already I'm getting a strong whiff of *wu wei* and *wu ming*, two fundamental Taoist concepts that bear on Erhard's philosophy. The first means "actionless action," the second means "without naming," or "nameless naming." Tao says that the Way never acts, yet nothing is left undone. Erhard is suggesting that the way to relax, that is, the way to do this something, is not to do it. This is sometimes good advice, but most of those in the audience, new to the notion, can't follow it. Some are even becoming angry with themselves for not being able to follow the directions and this simply compounds their problems since now they must overcome their anger at not being able to follow the directions as well as their inability to follow the directions. The ideal state of Taoism is one in which, in the words of one of the *Tao Te Ching*'s translators, people are innocent of knowledge and free of desire. But most of the people in the audience don't know they're already in that state. Since they don't know it, they're not in it. And even if they *knew* it, they wouldn't be in it because, as Lao-tzu, Freud, Erhard, and other "trend-setters" know, knowledge alone will get you nowhere. In fact, you don't need to get anywhere at all; you're already there, if only you would *experience* that that's where you are. Erhard experienced "where he was" in his wife's Mustang: "What I recognized," he is fond of saying, "is that you can't put it together. It's already together and what you have to do is experience it being together."

Now, up on stage, prowling about like a lynx, he tells us: "Thinking won't get you there, but most people don't think well enough to see that thinking doesn't work."

Erhard is beginning to reveal his aptitude for certain truths, and the audience knows this even if they hang on to those truths by only a slender cognitive thread. He's saying that you have to be pretty smart to realize how dumb you are or, to use his words, how like a "machine," a "Tube," you are, through which life passes like an undigested meal (somewhat like Gurdjieff's Instinctive Motor Men). Most people don't think well enough to realize that thinking can only get you to the station but not on the train.

Feelings can't get you there either, Erhard says. This is what many screamers, gropers, wailers, and confrontationalists have found out. Forget thinking, he says, forget feeling.

The first process that Erhard puts the audience through concerns experiencing to what extent you define yourself by your past and to what extent you characterize your past as good or bad, instead of as *is*. One's past just *is*, and Erhard tries to show the crowd, by having them invent different good and bad "pasts" for themselves with their eyes closed, that thinking of your past as good or bad has an effect on the present moment, and not a very beneficial one. People drag their pasts behind them—and he illustrates by walking about the stage pulling his canvas chair and metal music stand-qua-podium behind him and making an expression like he just ate his first raw littleneck clam. It's his intention to convince everyone that, in fact, the past can be completed so that it no longer intrudes on the present, preventing people from experiencing themselves. People, he says, are not inclined to believe that something—like one's past—can be made to disappear. But, he argues, if you would only "complete it," it would go away.

And with this, Erhard begins to wax psychoanalytic. There is no contentment or peace without first experiencing one's own history. History, as Joyce's Stephen Dedalus noted, is a nightmare from which he was trying to awake. Delmore Schwartz, the late American author and critic, noted that history was a nightmare during which he was trying to get some sleep. But one *must* awake. No ghosts, psychic or otherwise, can be slain in absentia and Erhard, on a mass scale, is seeking to summon them.

But to listen carefully here is to catch a dangerous note in Erhard's monologue; for all his brave talk about "experiencing through barriers," there is more than a touch of positive thinking in what he says. The process he has just put us through suggests that the past has little reality beyond our thoughts about it, that our thinking it is good or bad makes it so, that, in short, thoughts are *things*. But how can he suggest this when he has already warned us against thinking? Surely, there is more to "completing" one's past than mental exercises.

But Erhard has moved on, and engagingly so, dulling one's memory of the last moment's inconsistencies. Who would think to quibble with him about garbled messages when he has just called us all "assholes"? A man in the balcony gasps. Erhard has counted on there being at least one gasp in the house—quickly he lifts his head to the balcony and says, "I didn't say it was *bad* to be an asshole. Being an asshole isn't good or bad. It just is."

The gasp subsides into a widespread aah-ing of recognition. We *are* assholes. Of course! And the tricks we play to convince ourselves we aren't—they must be dealt with. The game of life is here and now, and one had better learn its rules, its immediacy, and learn to play it well and with some measure of irony and balance or there is no way at all to win. In Erhard's metaphor, people live in a "pea soup" existence where nothing can be clearly seen, in which it is laborious to move, and from which they imagine they can escape.

But the pea soup is *it!* There is nothing outside the great tureen of life! The only thing to be done is to clarify that murky experience. Bouillon? Broth? Chicken soup? Yes, that's it—chicken soup! Life-giving, orthopedic chicken soup!

Then it hits me. No, not the "It" you're supposed to "get" from the four-day *est* training. (I have never taken the training; my explanation—one Erhard himself could not object to—is that *my* "experience" of *est* is not taking it.) No, what hits me is the simple observation that Erhard is not speaking your standard nickle-dime psychobabble. He's bursting with *good* thoughts. He's bursting with *great* thoughts, borrowed, often with no collateral, from some of the great philosophical and psychological traditions and translated into a manic, convoluted spectacle. Now people don't have to go directly to Chuang-tsu or Wittgenstein or *The Interpretation of Dreams* or Krishnamurti or anybody. Werner has read the books for you. He not only used to sell the great books—he *is* the great books. Or at least the tables of contents. He's up there on stage and he's saying this is it! Don't look over our shoulder, he says, I'm talking to *you*, you asshole, pinch yourself because there's no way at all to get out of this dream, the one you're in right now and which you're trying to get out of by dreaming other dreams. He's giving you the Classic Comics version of the best cerebration that's been cerebrated, and he never even went to college!

Here's what Erhard knows: life is shitty. "Life stinks," he beams. "But it's not bad that life stinks. It just stinks. That's what is." A rational pessimism to rival Freud's, to out-Hobbes Hobbes. He's oneupping the giddy hawkers of cure by saying what every American sophisticate has begun to suspect—that there is *no* cure, after all. What comfort in mutually acknowledged despair! And so what if this new pessimism, so casually adopted, turns out to be no more than an urbane front for the same old optimism, the same old fascination with the self? So what if the phrase "Life stinks," uttered with the proper élan and at the proper moment in a lengthy monologue, has a way finally of denying its own message, is tantamount to saying "Life is good," hits the ear of the unconscious as a reassurance? So what? "Life stinks" sounds good, it's the right thing to say, it's what they feel in the ghettos of the world, isn't it?

No, Erhard's psychobabble is not the amorphous psychobabble of the streets and the dens of the human potential movement. It has more corners, twists and turns than the simple garden-variety "I've just got to be myself, let me get my head together" refrain. This is something different. This is *high* psychobabble! This is Deep Meaning cut so that people can wear it anywhere, a fashion for all seasons. This is the Banter of Big Ideas!

Erhard is a master of the paraphrase, saying everything half a dozen times in different ways. It is not in his interest to be any clearer, any more succinct, for it is easier to break down a person's or an entire audience's defenses by making them squirm with boredom and irritation. That forces *all* of their feelings more to the surface, so that their impatience with Erhard or his trainers is immediately blunted by that other feeling nudging in, that one had better listen because one *is* an asshole. It's no secret that everyone feels pretty bad "inside," that everyone is waiting to be told what to do, and *est* proves once again how easy it is to infantilize a group of people.

Erhard sometimes sounds like the offspring of Mr. Wizard and Miss Francis of "Ding Dong School." He tells the audience he loves them. He tells them, when they have closed their eyes at his instruction for a process, "Good, I'll give you ten more seconds to complete your past." And when they've opened their eyes, he says that was nice, that was very good.

In the rich atmosphere of momentousness that Erhard can ingeniously create, he proffers largely good advice on how to live with and inside of paradox instead of nervously taking sides on every issue; he is, truly, providing a third dimension, opening up a "space" for people to glimpse that cosmic perspective on their problems which is so hard to achieve in a cluttered life.

But then something else begins to creep into the atmosphere, like a poisonous vapor. It is the suggestion, at first faint but then gaining momentum, that he cannot see, or else can see but does not wish to convey, that one lives necessarily in a social, political, and economic world, and no retreat into the spiritual can alter that reality. One cannot, should not, turn the spotlights on the self only to plunge the world out there into darkness—because even that darkness is affecting you. That is why a certain Hassidic master, when he began to slip away into a spiritual ecstasy, would keep his eye on a clock in order to keep himself in this world.

But keeping oneself in the world, perceiving at every possible moment the connections between the self and society, between the spirit and politics—this was missing. Not that anyone in Symphony Hall's seats was likely to fall into a rapture and be carried irretrievably away onto the astral plane, but rather this: at one point, having brought up this country's national debt, Erhard asserted that there is "no way to experience the national debt, it doesn't really affect your life." Now, it is true that there are many sources of our suffering, and that many of them—perhaps all, ultimately—

lie within us, but the national debt is still very real. For one thing, it had something to do with the price of the tickets to this very event. Was Erhard making such an inane remark in the hope of diverting our attention from his own increasing prosperity, to which we were at that moment contributing? Probably not. But it is clear that, for all his wisdom, Erhard is making the mistake of teaching self-awareness as if it ought to exclude other sorts of awareness. The class orientation of his gospel comes through strongly when he announces in his endearing manner that "It's fun to be yourself. The self is fun to the self. The real self is actually satisfied. If you think you need something out there to be satisfied, you're in the wrong context."

Erhard obviously didn't think it was "fun just to be yourself" for the Third World—*est*'s work in prisons and among the disadvantaged implies a more practical orientation—but I recalled the impression I had registered when entering the hall that evening. Beyond the fact that almost everyone was smiling, a tolerable banality, they were virtually all well-dressed—even the disheveled had *style*—and healthy, and white, and well-educated. Not a black among them, only a couple of Latin Americans. It was not exactly the world. These were still the children of the dream who, having passed through their phase of political activism or maximum material comfort, had run smack into some private emptiness. *Est* does not fail to notice the quality of its following. One of its maxims is that life is three feet long and that those who do not want for basic needs can now be concerned with that "last quarter inch called satisfaction."

It could not be ignored: Erhard was still, years after Mind Dynamics and selling Fords, rooted in salesmanship. Only this time he was addressing those who were their own customers. And what they had sold themselves were the rinds of the American dream—the dream itself was no longer available—and then the rinds weren't enough and so they came to hear Erhard and perhaps take the training, which involved a new dream of completion.

Erhard had told them he wanted to "create a space to make this the most important night of your life" and they had dutifully closed their eyes when asked because, in fact, they were tired of dinner-and-a-show. And their expectation was that whatever Erhard could do for them now, and his trainers could do in the future, it could be done pretty quickly.

Erhard obliges by commenting in Symphony Hall that "As soon as you see you're stuck in the pea soup, it clears up. It just takes a while to manifest itself publicly." Although his message had on and off appeared to be that the process of enlightenment goes on forever, rather like portions of his monologues, the pitch was again subtly shifting. He had been intimating how incapable the audience was of experiencing themselves, had been rubbing their noses all along in their own stupidity and *now*, by some imaginative leap, was letting slip the suggestion that it wasn't so hard after all, that all one had to do was see the pea soup for what it was and—Presto!—clear chicken broth! He had gone from philosophical showman to psychobabbler in an instant. Self-awareness was suddenly as close as the nearest *est* trainer.

First he upsets that old applecart of the Conscious Self in Control by demonstrating that people's lives run *them*, and no one can argue with that assessment. Things don't look good; it's no easy matter putting all those apples back in place, particularly when so many are bruised. But wait— Erhard can't leave his audience in the lurch. He's got to promise them they'll be back on their feet in two weekends. So he does an about-face and begins talking as if the applecart hadn't been upset after all.

So what else is new? Instant regeneration is a motif common to countless therapies and religions. How does Erhard get away with it?

The answer is: because he's so damn *good* at what he does. His doctrine is, unlike that of Scientology, from which *est* partly derives, deliberately uncharacterizable. He has put an array of beliefs, religious impulses, and psychological theories into the blender and the result obscures its own composition. It becomes an "It" one "gets." In an increasingly post-literate age, it is hard to see through the ideological vanishing act. If you do criticize *est*, you simply haven't got "It." What is "It"? According to Erhard himself, "IT is you experiencing yourself without any symbology or any concept. Normally, I experience myself through my thoughts; I think who I am. Sometimes I experience myself through my body; I sense who I am. Sometimes I experience myself through my emotions; I feel who I am. Well, IT is you experiencing you directly without any intervening system."

But what does it mean to experience oneself without any symbology or concept? It makes no sense. Surely, there are mystical states which temporarily suspend those concepts and symbologies, but one cannot function in the world in such a state; these people have to go to work the next day! *Est* itself is an "intervening system"—a clever, elusive system, but a system nevertheless. The sophisticated marketplace does not want to buy an ideology so he packages it as nothing at all. He's a master of the intellectual airbrush. If the public takes to Pet Rocks, they'll absolutely love nothing. "Once you get It," he tells the crowd at another lecture, "you have to prove that you've got It. But proving you've got It means you haven't got It. So the only thing to do once you've got It is to give It up."

But "It" and the vocabulary of *est* tend to promote a

subtle ideology of indifference. While "space" may be a nice metaphor for a psychological state, the ethos of "I'm in my space and you're in your space, and that's okay" flattens out distinctions and reduces curiosity about the world and the complexity of the self to an attitude of haughty resignation. A culture that deposits virtually identical Howard Johnson's about the landscape, sparing travelers the shock of the unfamiliar, is a culture whose people eventually expect to encounter themselves in everyone they meet. *Est* stimulates that appetite for homogeneity.

The clinical psychologist at Lompoc prison in California who took *est* along with many prisoners there told Adelaide Bry, the author of one of the numerous and tedious "quickie" books on *est* published in 1976: "What I do now is simply suspend all judgment. Judgment is a voice in the back of my head and it still goes on but I don't allow it to affect my relationships." The implication that the decision not to judge is not a judgment becomes perilous in a group context, and reports of *est*onians' submission to Erhard's authority are disconcerting. Erhard's tight control over the activities of those who work and volunteer for him, and the religious sense of service that control inspires in underlings, amount to nothing less than the latest form of mass-ochism, Once exposé of *est* in *New Times* includes this anecdote:

On New Year's Day, for example, Erhard discovered that the downstairs washing machine in Franklin House had been left on, and worse—it had a safety pin in it. Naturally, this provoked the writing of yet another memo. "Werner wants you to locate the source of the above and then go through the process of cleaning that kind of thing up," an aide wrote. "This includes creating a policy to correct this situation from happening in

64

the future and also a determination of why this situation was not being supervised to enable its discovery by someone other than Werner." The new policy didn't work. Two weeks later, Erhard returned to Franklin House to discover a dysfunctional light bulb in the front porch light. "I don't believe it!" he shouted.

But the authoritarianism goes deeper. Employees are told to stay in communication with Werner about all their relationships, platonic or otherwise. In this way, *est* combines the best of both totalitarianism *and* the sexual revolution.

Erhard's response to an interviewer's question about the "tendency toward fanaticism" in *est* was eloquently circumspect:

There is that tendency in most of us to give up our own autonomy to someone else. . . . We like to give the person the opportunity to what we call, experience it out. The pattern, what we call mechanical behavior, *comes up* and the person becomes conscious of it. And by becoming conscious of it, it loses its power over them. So, when you say that you've seen people come out on both sides of the coin in *est*, we acknowledge *for sure* that that will happen. Whichever kind of pattern is most strong for the person, that's the one that they'll deal with first. We assume that they'll get to deal with the other one because the pendulum always swings the other way, eventually.

The note of concern for people's vulnerability to mechanical behavior is reassuring, but why then does Erhard insist on tactics such as instituting, on his return once from a trip to Japan, an exercise involving a daily hour of just "sitting" for all his employees?

The Russian-Greek mystic Gurdjieff at least put a sign over the door to his study at his Institute for the Harmonious Development of Man which read: IT IS USELESS TO PASS THROUGH THESE DOORS UNLESS YOU HAVE WELL-DEVELOPED CRITICAL FACULTIES. No such advice is offered to the *est*onians. Indeed, many *est*onians, pacified by their dose of enlightenment, refuse to look beyond the temporarily therapeutic experience into the darker side of Erhard's genius. One man who wrote a letter to the editor of a magazine that ran an investigative article on Erhard stated that *est* had changed his life and that as far as he was concerned questions of character were totally irrelevant.

There is no point in condemning *est* for giving people what they want, and in many ways what they truly need, but there is really something of Ibsen's *Peer Gynt* in the whole situation. The roguish, charming, and self-deceptive Peer travels about, at one point posing as a prophet whose surpassing virtue is that he "always tried to be Myself." He is soon hailed by the director of an insane asylum in Cairo as "A man who's himself!" The director, who himself is quite mad, introduces him to the inmates as "The Emperor of Revelation based on Self!" and then says of himself and the inmates what might equally describe spiritual acolytes of the seventies:

> We're ourselves and nothing but ourselves,
> We speed full sail ahead as ourselves,
> We shut ourselves up in a keg of self,
> We stew in our own juice, we seal ourselves up
> Hermetically with a bung of self
> And get seasoned in a well of self.
> We never consider anyone else;
> There are no thoughts nor sorrows outside our own;

We are ourselves in thought and in word,
Ourselves to the farthest, the uttermost edge.

Peer, although offended that these others should also consider themselves Gyntian Selves, discovers by the end of both
the play and his life that he too is an impostor. Heaven is of
course out of the question for him and, to his dismay, so is
Hell. He is too "mediocre": neither a man who was truly
himself nor even "A sinner in a magnificent way" who de-
serves Satan, he is to be melted down by the Button Molder
along with all the others who felt, not the extremes of passion, "But only a constant anxiety."

A few years ago, the only way to convene 2,612 liberal-
minded people would have been for a political rally or
demonstration. The event at Symphony Hall signified a clean
break with that recent past. Those who had once flirted with
the counterculture and change on a broader scale seemed
now to have given up their passion in order to begin some
slap-dash centripetal journey into the atomistic self. It was,
in many respects, a sorry scene, for it may be possible to say
of *est* what historian Donald Meyer has written in his book,
The Positive Thinkers, of American mind cure cults of the
last century:

> It was the genius of mind cure to discover how the
> weak might feel strong while remaining weak. They
> could get sick, then heal themselves. Becoming healthy
> became in itself an end, its own world and testimony to
> the nature of the world. Mind cure's passivity with re-
> spect to charity, reform and style, repeated in its psy-
> chology, followed by necessity if health was to constitute
> just this end-in-itself, and not, as ordinarily, simply a
> condition allowing pursuit of ends and life generally.
> . . . What mind cure offered by way of action was

precious because it was action, and at the same time
action not touching the world. Feelings of strength were
induced that never had to be tested against other
strength. It was strength that did not have to overcome
dependency.

Est may be an amphetamine for the spirit, but it's a Mickey
Finn for the body politic.

A few years ago, Erhard told a journalist that he didn't
think the world needed *est* because "the world already is,
and that's perfect."

"If nobody needs it," the journalist asked, "why do you do
it?"

"I do it," Erhard replied, "because I do it, because that's
what I do." Erhard by now may actually believe this tauto-
logical nonsense, this misapplied Zen, but his soul is getting
restless. Life is shitty but, as he's finding out, so is celebrity.
His nervousness came out at Symphony Hall that night, but
couched in the candor his followers are so apt to take at face
value.

"When I was starting *est*," he addressed the audience, "I
wrestled with the thought that I was just on an ego trip. But
then I realized I was *obviously* on an ego trip and that it's
egotistic to think you can do anything *without* your ego."
Much laughter here. "Now that I'm a public figure, I sometimes worry that I'll never get to see people closer than forty
feet up. I worried that I'd lose all my friends. But now I
realize that I've got nothing to give up, nothing to worry
about. I have a completely and wholly satisfying relationship
with each of you."

Erhard was so full of the need to be well thought of (at a
distance of forty feet), so in need of knowing that it was
okay to be powerful, famous, and bright, that it was hard not
to grow a little uneasy in my seat. When the guru begins

asking for his subjects' approval, one begins to suspect that he's still in some kind of pea soup.

He took out and read a letter from an *est* graduate that began "I love you, Werner" and ended *"est* is brilliant, amazing," and with that Jack Rosenberg sprang from the stage and strode up the center aisle of Symphony Hall to vigorous applause, a spotlight full on him, with all the pomp and favorable circumstance of a high school valedictorian.

CO-COUNSELING:

The Sharpest People We Know

ESTONIANS ARE ADVISED by their trainers to respond when friends ask them about *est* by explaining that everyone has his or her own experience of it, and that trying to describe it "would be like trying to describe the taste of an orange to someone who has never tasted one." Be that as it may, he who has yet to taste an orange may have nonetheless tasted a lemon, grapefruit, or tangerine and therefore be in a position to learn something about the taste of an orange by comparison. But *est* is to its followers a rare fruit that could only be demeaned by comparison.

Similarly, co-counselors refuse to talk much about their activities. They sometimes behave as if they were hoarding military secrets. But the rumors are that they are extremely happy. They hug a lot. They cry or laugh loudly at the odd-

est times. At an Avis Rent-A-Car office, I run into someone I knew vaguely in high school. He's in co-counseling and
says it's beautiful, says something about "the blossoming of
the human being." One veteran co-counselor will talk about
it, but adds, shrugging, with the air of a Defense Department
spokesperson explaining the budget to a gathering of college
undergraduates: "Frankly, I'm worried that you'll misrepre-
sent co-counseling. I don't think you can understand what
I'm talking about."

One woman who was a co-counselor for three years describes the "semi-official technique" for recruiting new co-
counselors: "You're not supposed to tell people they need it,
and you're supposed to *not* talk about it a lot, and treat it
like something you have that they don't, and that it's real
special. The first few times people ask you about it, you tell
them nothing. You just say it's something you do. Then they
begin to ask you more and more about it each time, and
you're supposed to think about where they're at and what
they want to hear. You drop them bits of information. You
figure out what's missing in their lives and work on that."

It's an attitude that calls to mind Freud's advice on how
best to present psychoanalysis to the uninitiated in one of his
New Introductory Lectures on Psychoanalysis from 1916:
"The best plan would be for you to conceal your superior
knowledge altogether. If that is no longer possible, limit
yourself to saying that, so far as you can make out, psychoanalysis is a special branch of knowledge, very hard to
understand and to form an opinion on." Fifty years ago,
public resistance to ideas about unconscious behavior was
such that Freud's reticence, however condescending, was
justified; but in today's less suspicious public atmosphere,
particularly in America, one wonders about the need for a
conspiratorial silence on therapeutic matters.

While Transcendental Meditation, Transactional Analysis,

est and a host of other cures preoccupy the media, Re-evaluation Counseling—better known simply as co-counseling—has been virtually unpublicized for the more than twenty years of its existence. Co-counselors prefer word-of-mouth publicity only and on that basis co-counseling has become a discreet international movement claiming co-counseling communities from Argentina to Zaire. Most co-counselors—a term which describes all followers since one both counsels and in turn is counseled in this highly egalitarian therapy—subscribe to an unwritten policy that only those who are interested in becoming co-counselors should be told much of anything about it. This can be very disconcerting to the casual outsider, particularly if he happens to know that Re-evaluation Counseling founder Harvey Jackins's answer to the question "Whom should we invite into the co-counseling community and classes?" is: "The sharpest people we know."

Considering such secrecy, one might expect co-counselors to be protecting from public view arcane shamanistic rituals or some psychic slave trade like Sun Myung Moon's Unification Church. But in theory, and to a large extent in practice, co-counseling is a far from ominous cult that participates in its own unique way in the ideals of the era of feeling. Unlike *est*, with its freeze-dried Zen, its boot-camp atmosphere, its seductive "It" one "gets" ("understanding," remember, is only the "booby prize"), co-counseling is built on supportiveness and mutual appreciation. No one is called a turkey or an asshole in co-counseling; from the start the very best is assumed about the individual, and love, cooperation, and enthusiasm are emotional staples. Unlike *est*, at no time is anyone prevented from going to the bathroom (although the use of caffeine, tobacco, alcohol, and drugs is prohibited during class meetings). Co-counseling's lifeblood is optimism. Within the first fifteen minutes of an introductory class, we were told by the teacher that we were "all geniuses."

Unlike meditation, there are no "mystical" skills to practice. Unlike psychoanalysis and psychotherapy, co-counseling costs nominally for weekly group classes and nothing at all for individual peer co-counseling, which can go on indefinitely. Furthermore, it is resolutely non-authoritarian; there is no privileged knowledge, no analytic interpretation. The basic therapeutic skill is trained listening to another's talk, and the ability to reverse roles and talk freely in return; to become a "one-way counselor" and not, in turn, let oneself be counseled by one's peers is frowned upon as authoritarian.

And unlike the self-help culture, co-counseling recognizes the limitations of auto-enlightenment, then trusts that ordinary, unprofessional people can help you find your way. This notion was at the heart of co-counseling's humble origins back in the early fifties. It is a story recited at most co-counseling introductory meetings. Harvey Jackins, a B.A. in mathematics who later became a labor organizer in Seattle in the forties until blacklisted, was confronted by a friend named Charlie, who had just lost his job and split up with his wife. He ended up at Harvey's in an extremely agitated state. Harvey asked Charlie what was wrong and Charlie broke down in front of him and began to cry. Harvey told him not to cry, but Charlie kept on for a long time, day and night, until Harvey made him stop because he had to return to work. When Harvey came back, Charlie started crying again. This went on for a week or two, after which time Charlie began to shake. He then shook for a week or two while Harvey looked on, now unable or unwilling to interrupt his friend's copious catharsis. The shaking gave way to a spell of yawning, during which Charlie kept repeating the same life story, and then the yawning became laughter. Eventually there was a breakthrough; Charlie seemed to recover and went back with his wife. Harvey was impressed. The guy was cured! And Harvey wasn't even a shrink—all he had had to do was pay sympathetic attention to Charlie and eventually everything worked itself out.

Out of this experience grew the co-counseling "theory." What is most strikingly different about co-counseling as one reads through Harvey Jackins's several books is its insistence on the importance of intelligence, logic, and rationality. In a time when Feelings, and Deep Feelings particularly, are thought of as the lost paradise to which all must return—and surely as much unnecessary distress and confusion are caused by this notion as are alleviated—co-counseling, more than most alternative therapies, appears to concern itself with the complex relations between logic and emotion. If *est*, Primal Therapy, and other "nonrational" programs treat intelligence as an impediment to the recovery of repressed pain and its re-integration, Jackins sees it as indispensable to growth.

For Jackins, human intelligence is "the ability to respond to each different situation in the environment with a fresh, new, accurate response." It is precisely this faculty, rather than that of "feeling," accoridng to Jackins, that is re-pressed by the individual as he or she undergoes a trauma. The trauma, or "hurt" in Jackins's vocabulary, is the source of dysfunction in humans and it "leaves the information input during the hurt experience in the form of a rigid, com-pulsive pattern of feeling and behavior rather than as useful information." So far, so Freud; this is Jackins's own thumb-nail version of repression.

But at this point Jackins takes off in the direction of the old cathartic theories of healing. "Restimulation"—that is, the repetition of that compulsive pattern established as a response in the past, a term borrowed from Scientology, with which Jackins was acquainted in the fifties—must be avoided in favor of its therapeutic alternative, discharge. The concept and act of discharge hold a prominent place in co-counseling theory and practice, much like the use of "Primal" in Primal Therapy. Discharge describes a set of processes—"undoubtedly very complex," Jackins allows—involving the release of tension, and these processes are characterized by the "outward indications of crying with tears, trembling with perspiration, laughter, angry noises with violent movements, yawning, and lively talking." When a co-counselor discharges, he disrupts the old patterns and has "re-evaluations"—or insights—that enable him to regain the ability to "act logically at all times." To help one along the road to intelligence and rationality, Jackins provides the following advice, from his small handbook called *Quotes from Harvey Jackins*, a Mao-inspired attempt to endow excerpts from Jackins's books, letters, and conversations with the flavor of immortality: "Act as if you were already completely rational, which does not mean to pretend that the way you *act* is already completely rational." "The only option for survival," he warns in the same booklet, "is to get smart."

Co-counselors strive toward "awareness," which is a higher order of intelligence, and also toward recapturing "zestfulness." Zest is to co-counseling what The Absence of Significant Blocking Pain is to Primal Therapy and original sin is to a good Catholic—it is "the natural feeling of a human being," just as "the natural relationship with other human beings is love and cooperation."

"Appreciation" is one of the things you do a lot of to recover that original Zest. Appreciation takes two basic forms in co-counseling. In general, co-counseling encourages everyone to appreciate everyone else, since this is part of loving, sharing, and cooperation. *Est* "acknowledges" you; co-counseling "appreciates" you. In the co-counseling quarterly, *Present Time*, published in Seattle, there is a regular feature of notes and comments called "Appreciation," in which, for instance, someone from Olympia, Washington, writes: "I would like to express how much I appreciate Del Oakes for his aware, loving attention that has turned out to mean so much to me this past year."

The Complete Appreciation of Oneself Without Reservation is a therapeutic technique used to induce discharge of "chronic distress patterns." It was discovered during the evolution of co-counseling that clients were unable to get at certain deeper distresses easily and that the way to stir them up was to have the client appreciate himself "out loud, without any reservations"; by having a person deliver in front of a group unqualified and flattering statements about himself that naturally contradict his concealed misgivings and doubts, those misgivings and doubts make their presence more strongly felt.

In *The Human Situation*, Jackins instructs co-counselors to appreciate themselves "with appreciative, positive words," "a proud exultant posture," "a pleased, happy expression on your face," and to do so to your co-counseling group, your co-counselor, friend or friends, family, the casual passerby, God, even the mirror, steering wheel, and fence post. Why? "You will discharge," he writes. "You will act rationally. You will hold to a good direction. You will emerge from your old dependencies. You will take charge of your life. . . . When such a person can be convinced to try a direction such as 'Daddy was always a joy' uttered in a bright tone of voice, discharge begins immediately."

To prove this theory correct at an introductory class, the leader, a cherubic woman in her early twenties who giggled excessively, asked for a volunteer. A young man stood up before the group of thirty and, both of his hands now in the grip of the leader and her aide, was asked to tell the group what his best qualities were. "Well," he began tentatively, "I think I'm intelligent and I'm a generous person, and when I want to do something, I keep doing it until I'm good at it."

"Okay," the leader smiled, "but say it again without the 'I think.' Be confident. Brag about yourself!"

The victim began again, but still in a soft voice, faltering.

The leader giggled and told him to say it louder, more positively, to say he was fantastic. "Here," she suggested, "put your thumbs in your lapels like this."

The man did so and began again, "I am fantastic! I am the best!" But as he said these things, of course he began to laugh himself.

The leader began to laugh joyfully. The leader's aide began to laugh. A bearded man in overalls sitting on the carpet, who also happened to be a co-counseling teacher, began to laugh. They were all "discharging." And now, the leader pointed out, so was the young man who had just said all those things about himself. He was "discharging" too! Then the leader asked all of us to pair off and begin bragging to each other.

Just as Jackins believes that throughout life, one is always in the position of either a client or counselor—either being listened to or listening—so it is expected that discharge will continue indefinitely since, as Jackins says, "We do not yet know if an adult, or, for that matter, a child, can fully and completely recover *all* of their inhibited intelligence and zestful capacity for living." Yet on this issue, Jackins experiences some confusion, for elsewhere, in *Quotes from Harvey Jackins*, he has this to say: "Discharge, discharge, discharge, and again discharge. Distress *can* be exhausted, *can* be discharged completely, leaving no trace. It is the counselor's responsibility to see that this is done." Sharing this optimism, one co-counselor expects "to be in co-counseling the rest of my life, or until the world's cleaned up and I don't have to deal with new distresses—and it *will* be cleaned up, but not in the next twenty years."

The format in which distress patterns are "counseled out" is both group and individual. A co-counselor may attend his group of between fifteen and twenty people once a week as long as he likes after completing the initial sixteen-week program at a cost of seventy dollars. The emphasis, however, is on individual co-counseling, a relationship with an untrained peer that involves at least one session a week in person or, as circumstances warrant, over the phone. During each session, one of the two counsels the other for a prearranged period of time, often an hour, and then they switch for the same amount of time. The counselor is directed to give his client "free attention," or "slack," performing a kind of vigil, a version of Carl Rogers's "unconditional positive regard." The counselor, according to *The Fundamentals of Co-Counseling Manual*, should be neither suggestive nor interpretive; should neither react emotionally to the client's monologue nor on the other hand seem indifferent; should not interrupt discharge, and should be courteous in tone, manner, and attitude.

Co-counselors are expected to refrain at all times from socializing with each other outside of their co-counseling activities, although inevitably in such an informal framework, romantic attachments occur and are exploited. In one instance, it is reported that a woman in California was blackballed from co-counseling for sleeping with a married co-counselor. But incidents like this are rare, and co-counseling is basically a friendly international constellation of communities. Any co-counselor passing through a strange city in which a co-counseling community exists may look up a member and get some counseling. It is in a sense one large nomadic therapeutic coterie in which discharge is as close as the nearest phone.

Because of Harvey Jackins's activist background, co-counseling possesses a political and social character rare among therapeutic organizations. Although officially nonpolitical and interested only in what one co-counselor calls "human emergence," co-counseling is also deeply concerned about eliminating racism and sexism and in expanding its sphere of influence to include the Third World. In fact, co-counseling's therapeutic goals are seen simultaneously as social ones. The rigidity of the social structure in America, which stands in opposition to human intelligence, is perceived as the sum of just so many rigid individual distress patterns. Deep distress patterns repeatedly restimulated in oppressed peoples insure their continued submission. For an individual to renounce his obligations as a citizen and a political force in his pursuit of responsibility is, for Jackins, "the most irrational role of all." Jackins's writing is sprinkled with exhortations to transform helplessness into participation in social processes. "As we find ways to discharge and eliminate all the patterns of racism, sexism, adultism towards children, of nationalism, of prejudice towards the physically handicapped, and all the other insidious viewpoints of oppression," Jackins once said in a workshop, "it will become crystal clear to all of us that ALL MEN ARE SISTERS."

One would not expect a politically committed therapy to envelope itself in notions about the primacy of merely "feeling" or to legislate the kind of zealous intimacy that in countless fly-by-night therapies has come to seem like too great a protest against its disappearance. And co-counseling does not, *in theory*, do this. Jackins argues that intelligence and logic, not "feelings," are the guide to action. If they are good feelings, he says, enjoy them, but don't be controlled by them. If they are bad feeings, feel them but don't be guided by them either. He has this saying, that when it's time to take out the garbage, don't discharge on it, just take out the garbage. Good feelings are *not* the goal of co-counseling.

At last, then, an indigenous American therapy, it seems, that is immune to the Feel Good Hypothesis, to the culture's call for presweetened familiarity. At last, a psychological movement that uses its head, that lets it all hang out precisely so that it can be put back to hang properly where it belongs. One is certain, reading Jackins, that he is intuitively sensitive to the fallacy of feeling, to the perils of exhibitionism disguised as liberation. He warns against inflicting on other people how loudly one can yell or swear. Wrecking furniture in the act of discharging is out and so, according to the books, is engaging "embarrassedly or defensively . . . in embraces in situations where such embraces will not be understood or to blindly try to impose such closeness on others."

While Americans in Primal chambers and on weekend catharses across the country are achieving ever higher octaves, Jackins coolly observes that the level of discharge is not the same as its importance, that expressions of grief are not necessarily more important than laughter or angry speech. While Primal-type therapies and much of the "therapeutic" advice doled out to readers in self-help books impose a conceptual split between thought and feeling in order to dispose of the former, Jackins seems to want to separate them in order to show each of them in its place. In one of his poems—whose rather humble execution does not necessarily detract from the validity of its thought—he writes: "I act by thought and logic/I just feel the way I feel/I don't confuse these separate things/Nor wind them on one reel."

But does co-counseling, de facto, live up to the expectations raised by its theory? One woman in her late twenties joined for a year while she was also in psychoanalytic therapy. Therefore she was not relying entirely on co-counseling for psychological growth, and in fact saw it as "something else to try," as she had previously sampled yoga and meditation. "It was very supportive," she says, "and that says something. And it's cheap. As one of my teachers is fond of saying to each class, it costs less than a movie in town, and it's usually more interesting. But my personal opinion is that co-counseling can lead to a lot of avoidance. If you're getting close to a highly charged issue, you can just change co-counselors. It doesn't go into why people get themselves in bad situations in the first place."

Another woman, Martha, a long-time observer of co-counseling in New York and a friend of many co-counselors, offers similar sentiments. "The peer notion is good and so is co-counseling's breakdown of the authoritarian aspect. And to see anti-sexism and anti-racism in direct connection with psychological awareness is good. I think people do get better, more mellowed out, more cheerful. It makes the tight, repressed person more productive. But I don't think it helps the truly depressed. It just doesn't go very deep."

The question is, to what extent does co-counseling address symptoms and rearrange a person's demeanor while leaving the sources of distress undisturbed? To what extent does co-counseling, despite its internally publicized prohibition against imposed intimacy, offer not so much a rigorous analysis of the self as precisely that variety of programmatic, mutual admiration—or "appreciation"—that so easily pre-empts real transformation? Does it simply offer the repressed an opportunity to reveal a gratifyingly risqué fringe of undergarment, thereby making it even easier to remain fully attired?

"The bulk of co-counseling people I know," says Martha, "are overintellectualized and underfeeling. Co-counseling corrects that imbalance. These people need official recognition of their emotional side. The collective aspect is important, particularly for Marxists," she continues, alluding to co-counseling's popularity among leftists. "Co-counseling is kosher for sixties radicals; it allows them to remain fully political. There is the co-counseling extended family, the sense of ongoing relatedness.

"Yet this secondary, familial affection makes the lack of primary feeling even more striking. I know two men in co-counseling who, when they greet each other, hug stiffly, perfunctorily, like a military salute. They're taking something good—the idea of men loving each other—and programming it. They really do love each other, but the physical manifestation is awkward, the shoulders don't relax into the hug. That sort of sums up the poignancy of co-counseling."

According to Martha, the emotional manifestations are often no more convincing than the physical. "Co-counseling dodges the depths. It just turns out that regular people aren't expert enough to really help you significantly. This business of discharge drives me crazy; it takes laughter and crying out of its real natural context and mechanizes it. There's an enormous amount of inappropriate affect going around. It's as if co-counselors are so grateful for strong feelings, regardless of the situation, that they must discharge them whenever possible.

"Co-counseling levels the distinctions between kinds of intimacy. Let me explain: co-counseling's critique of American society is absolutely correct—people in the WASP, technological culture here are raised like zombies. Things that most Jews and Italians take for granted—being open and loving—get lost on the culture at large. People *are* deeply distressed. So co-counseling is speaking to a real need, and it is politically correct in the process.

"But the theory has no richness. Co-counselors don't seem

able to live to the natural extremes of distress and joy—instead of an intense experience, co-counseling gives you a laughing fit. It's a bizarre trade-off. I must repeat that many people seem improved by it, but co-counseling is deeply impersonal in some sense. Americans believe that life is redeemable through education, and co-counseling is a prime example of that theory. It's like an auto mechanics course in feeling."

One middle-aged professor, who fled wartime Germany to come to this country, sees it differently. He has been in co-counseling for three years and finds it, compared to his experience in traditional psychotherapy in the sixties, more flexible (as one who lost several friends to German concentration camps, he was initially attracted to co-counseling's non-authoritarianism). For him, co-counseling has provided a greater sense of control, and he perceives no trace of exhibitionism in his particular group. "Back when I joined in 1973, there was more acting out of people's fantasies of a beautiful world of loving, sharing people, and all of that. Co-counselors used to hug all the time in the street. Now it's more sophisticated and people are more sensitive to whether others want to be embraced."

For Jessie, a woman in her early twenties who spent over three years in co-counseling, one of them as a co-counseling teacher, the therapy had soured. What had begun to annoy her was what she calls co-counseling's "no-fault attitude." In co-counseling, as in any remotely effective therapy, the individual is encouraged to assume responsibility for his distress and not perceive it as caused by a conspiracy of circumstance or other people. But then in co-counseling a curious thing happens. One is told that there is a "clear distinction" between one's distress pattern and oneself; that, in Jackins's phrase, "A pattern is no more YOU than an unpleasant mess which has stuck to the bottom of your shoe is you." Of course, while one presumes that behind a person's neurotic behavior lies the potential for a different sort of behavior, and that therefore a "distress pattern" is not ineluctably you, it is foolish to promote the idea that while you *are* drawing on obsolete responses, it is not you who is doing so. Who else could it possibly be? The consequences of this sort of psychobabble can be severe; once a person begins to think of his distress as something he *has*, the process of disclaiming responsibility sets in. As soon as a person sees the distress as an object to be dislodged or scraped away, rather than as the way that person is and what he does, whether or not he will always act this way, he begins to imagine that it can be totally removed to expose something bright and virginal underneath. When the teacher at a co-counseling introductory lecture said to the group that once you are able to discharge old distress patterns "you get back to the inherent, natural human being," I raised my hand and asked her exactly what she meant by "natural human being."

"Don't you believe," she asked me, "that underneath your distress and hurt there is a loving, cooperative human being?"

"No," I replied. "I think that underneath the bad patterns are other patterns. They may be much better patterns of acting or responding, or they may even be worse, but they are just more patterns. What does 'inherent, natural human being' mean, anyway? The child the moment he or she is born? A week after? At the age of two? Why do you think that underneath it all is some perfect little individual? Do you have any evidence for believing there is?"

At that point, another woman who had been in co-counseling for a while told me quietly and with the slightly impatient tone of an instructor who wants to restore order to her classroom: "Well, that's just an assumption that co-counseling makes."

I seemed to be the only one in the room who had any

doubts that all one had to do was discharge the bad stuff until there was nothing left but the good stuff. What co-counseling so cleverly manages to do here is to dangle in front of one's nose the importance of taking responsibility for the distress—which is certainly something we all would truly like to do, however difficult the process—and then, once the audience is sufficiently captivated by the challenge and perhaps squirming a bit in their seats, co-counseling ignores the implications of that sticky problem and substitutes for it a more pleasing Rousseauian illusion, that everything we suffer from is just something, some piece of shit, a social turd we happened to step in, and that there is, once one changes shoes, not much to worry about.

In a June 1973, co-counseling workshop, the question was asked, "How do you appreciate Mr. Nixon?" The teacher responded: "You remember that the person is okay, but let him know that what he is doing is not all right. Let him know that he needs to cut out the stupid things he is doing; that isn't invalidating him. We have inherent affection for other human beings, but don't mince around with the patterns." It is ironic that a therapy so politically conscious would make such a distinction between what a public figure does and what he is. What's the sense of "appreciating" a president's character, which one has no firsthand contact with, while minimizing his actions, the very things which most affect us?

So what Jessie discovered in co-counseling was that what was at first her responsibility was soon not her fault and before long became nothing less than virtue. "Co-counseling bestows on you a halo of goodness, so nothing's your fault. Teachers, when interviewing prospective clients, tend to process anything the client says which disagrees with co-counseling as '*their* distress.' Co-counseling is heavily into not criticizing—it normally assumes a problem is not your fault, but the result of someone else's distress pattern. So in practice a lot of games are reinforced. For instance, it was easy for me as a teenager to get things by playing the little girl and acting more stupid than I was. I knew I was doing it, but didn't like that trait in myself. Yet co-counseling encouraged it by 'appreciation.' I eventually got into pretty bad shape because of co-counseling, and I *had* to leave.

"I went into the publishing business in New York, ready to appreciate everybody and be appreciated in turn, but I discovered that life is more complex. It's not always good that it's like that, but that's the way it is. Guys kept hitting on me sexually, and I was totally unprepared for it. I was too naïve. I had counseled off *all* my defenses!"

Although Jessie's youth was undoubtedly also a factor in her experiences, what good is a therapy, particularly one so resolutely anti-sexist, that rendered her naïve and helpless in the face of actual sexism? "This business about how all humans are basically good," she says, "—well, I'm sorry. I've already seen too much to believe it. By the age of twenty-two or twenty-five or twenty-seven, people aren't walking around any more saying 'I want most of all not to hurt anybody.' They're just trying to survive. Yet co-counseling doctrine is strict here; there's absolutely no discussion about its premises, about whether all people are good.

"And this appreciation *is* manipulation At one point I had grown so used to the mutual endorsement that goes on that I didn't think I was able to relate with anyone outside of co-counseling. Whenever I met outsiders I thought: 'I'm honest—you're fucked up.' Now I can account for human error. No more saying, 'That's just my distress pattern.'

"After I left co-counseling, no one from co-counseling ever came up to me and said, 'Gee, I see that you're leaving because your lifestyle is no longer compatible with co-counseling,' or, 'I see that you don't need it any more.' They all assume it was just another distress pattern that made me leave. Co-counseling's rigidity is pervasive. A number of teachers in this area only counsel for a living and do nothing else, and they're a little out of touch with the outside world. A whole part of co-counseling that blew me away constantly were the professions of love and admiration that were totally devoid of social contact, totally devoid of practical experience with people."

Ruth, not herself a co-counselor, but a friend of many, illustrated this last peril with one anecdote. A couple of years ago, a friend of hers, a Eastern European Marxist sociologist, had come to Brandeis University to write her doctoral thesis. Brandeis is the hub of the co-counseling community in the Boston area and it happened that she was assigned as thesis advisor, a professor there who had brought co-counseling to Boston after encountering it in California while on leave in 1970. He suggested to her that she join a group of thesis writers who regularly convened to discuss their work. Thinking this a good idea, she arrived the next day to find a crowd of graduate students hugging each other. She stood at the door, bewildered, until one graduate student approached her and exclaimed, "You're not hugging us!"

"No, I'm not," she replied. "I'm not hugging you because I don't know you and I have no feelings for you."

"Well," she was told, "that must be the source of your difficulties in writing your thesis. You don't have trust."

Eventually, the group members paired off in co-counseling style, and the Marxist was chosen by her advisor. They sat facing each other, holding hands; she began to talk abstractly about her thesis, her eyes wandering upward. The advisor, according to co-counseling's emphasis on good eye contact, strained to follow hers, at one point leaving his chair in a half-crouch. Annoyed by his optical pursuit, she found it hard to think straight, a symptom promptly identified by him as a distress pattern. Then she began to overhear other pairs and it seemed that each time a graduate student expressed some difficulty with his or her thesis, the interlocutor would respond, "Your thesis is great. It's going to make a contribution to world knowledge."

Appalled, the Marxist confronted her professor in his office the next day and told him that what she had heard the day before was ridiculous and, in addition, harmful. Not everyone's thesis, after all, could be a contribution to world knowledge. "You're not preparing people for reality," she said.

"You're talking out of false bourgeois consciousness," he replied.

Ruth had another friend she lost to co-counseling, out West. She was "the smartest person I'd ever met before co-counseling," but she returned from the Coast with an entirely new personal style. She laughed and yawned dramatically when anxious, and had developed an odd cackle. Once, at a large dinner party, she and another co-counselor suddenly clasped hands over the table, their eyes beginning to tear, muttered that they could not co-counsel there and, to the surprise of those present, ran off upstairs in the middle of the main course to discharge. "It's mad," Ruth explains. "They mechanize intimacy and call it spontaneity. They run love with a stop-and-start button."

Even some people suspicious of co-counseling's often fatuous practices are nonetheless seduced by it. As Jessie says, "Co-counseling meets certain needs fast. We're all walking around dying to hear we look okay, that we're nice, smart, and good. Co-counseling gives you that right away, in the first class. When I was a teacher, it was quite unbelievable to me how easily I could get through to even the cynics."

As an example of co-counseling's technique for dealing with pessimists, Jessie recalled a person who took exception to Harvey Jackins's belief that we don't have to die, certainly not until we're one hundred forty years old or thereabouts. As Jackins writes in *The Human Situation*, "My guess is that the mechanism of aging and death can be eliminated." Although it is probably true that a rationally lived life generally favors longevity, Jackins takes it further—right up to the serious consideration of immortality as a feature of the "natural, inherent human being." The story goes that Jackins's interest in deathlessness began one day when his kids asked him, "Daddy, do you have to die?" Jackins replied that he did and his kids started crying and wouldn't stop. So Jackins thought it over and thought maybe people didn't have to die and began trying to recruit scientists to support his belief. A co-counseling poster reads: "The way to stay young is not to grow old!"

"Talk about meeting a lot of people's needs, my friend," Jessie comments. "Anyway, when I was a teacher, if someone said to me, 'How can you believe that we never die?' I would ask him to come up to the front and I would take his hand and I would tell him to try saying, 'I never want to die.' That might produce some discharge. And if he said, 'But Harvey's theory is bullshit!' I would say, still holding his hand, 'When was the first time you were given some bullshit, who first sold you a bill of goods when you were a child, who does that remind you of?'" As in *est* and Primal Therapy, the trick is to avoid addressing the intellectual content of a criticism, and instead to exploit it as an example of "not getting It" or "Primal Pain" or "distress patterns." Which is odd, for a therapy whose guiding theory exalts the use of rational intelligence.

At the introductory class I attended, I spoke independently with two men in their thirties who were trying to decide whether they wanted to join co-counseling. One had been through five years of psychotherapy but was not satisfied he had overcome his difficulties with authority figures. I pointed out to him that co-counseling, with its peer-orientation and mutual massage, would probably not give him much of an opportunity to work on authority problems since the therapy itself was in flight from those problems by presuming that virtually anybody was equally able to help virtually anybody else. Of course, I pointed out, it was equally hard to work out authority problems with a psychotherapist one didn't respect. I told him I thought there were probably alternatives, but co-counseling, with its impatience to praise everyone indiscriminately, might not be effective at helping one negotiate real authority in the real world. He nodded more or less, added that he thought co-counseling theory, as it had been explained by the leader, sounded "awfully pat." But when I spoke with him at the end of the class, he had decided to join.

The other man was recently divorced. He told me that co-counseling seemed "sappy" and he wasn't sure what he was going to do. Fifteen minutes later, he too signed up.

There is ample cause to believe that most co-counselors have positive experiences. But positive experiences are not always the ones that force the issue of personal growth, and co-counseling is a comfortable refuge for the disappointed. One of its delicate deceptions is its messianic quality. Jackins has written that co-counselors "tend to think of themselves as inhabitants of a 'rational island' of humans whom they are helping to pull up out of the sea of irrationality in which people and civilization are struggling." Countless co-counselors write letters to *Present Time* expressing the same sentiments as a woman from Ann Arbor, who jotted this note to the organization quarterly: "Got the *Present Time* with the write-up of the Liberation Workshops today. It made me cry. I am here getting ready to help you save the world." Eventually, according to Jackins, the gradual improvement in the lives of succeeding generations under the influence of Re-evaluation Counseling may make "the great irrational threats . . . of war, prejudice, overcrowding and starvation" into "historical curiosities." This is reminiscent of L. Ron Hubbard's goal of "clearing the planet" through Scientology. Co-counseling's long-range goal is the complete conversion of society to intelligent behavior, and naturally co-counseling is the only medium for this transformation; as Jackins is recorded as saying in *Quotes*, "Being invited into Fundamentals classes should be regarded as being elected to The National Academy of Sciences rather than as visiting a supermarket or hooking up to a public utility."

Just as naturally, co-counseling suffers from a disquieting xenophobia; it "firmly insists" (although it is not always able to enforce this rule) that co-counseling not be mixed with any other therapy or psychology. Jackins substantiates such a dictum by claiming that co-counseling is "by now a rich, complex, highly integrated system of thought." He returns again and again in his writings to the importance and elegance of his theory. He ascribes to it precision and flexibility. It is immune to "anarchist" solutions and the idea that "spontaneity is sufficient" on the one hand; on the other, he says his theory offers no "pat" answers. Yet the "elegance" of his theory is continually undermined by clichés. His chapter on "The Source of Damage" in *The Human Side of Human Beings* begins, "*We get hurt*. Just that, *we get hurt*," and then proceeds to reduce all human distress and irrationality to the problem of "hurt." No provision is made to account for the specific origins of different kinds of "hurt"; why, for instance, some children and adults are hurt more than others by the same external trauma, why some people respond to hurt by becoming paranoid or schizophrenic, too manic or too withdrawn. Just as Martha claimed that co-counseling leveled distinctions of intimacy, so does it level distinctions of psychological disturbance (except for a rather simplistic distinction between "latent distress patterns" and more serious, intractable "chronic distress patterns'). Jackins admits that co-counseling does not yet have the resources to handle the "deeply distressed," yet he can go on to assert in a pamphlet entitled *A New Kind of Communicator*, ". . . the cardinal fact that no problem between people is so tough that it will not resolve if counseling is applied to it."

Curiously, co-counseling attempts to distinguish itself from touchy-feely therapies by allying itself with rationality and logic, yet provides its clients with a theoretically and practically sanctioned opportunity to "discharge" old hurt without interpretive interruption; under these conditions, any amount of "feeling" is likely to be considered therapeutic whether or not it is actually accompanied by insight. Jackins argues that if a distressed baby is simply allowed to cry without interference from a mother who maintains a positive, caring regard, the effects of the trauma will be canceled out. He is probably right that short-circuiting a child's discharge may create yet more problems, but there is, on the other hand, no evidence that catharsis alone does all the therapeutic work.

One of Jackins's books is littered with childish drawings that reify abstractions like mind, feelings, distress patterns, and experience as arrows, circles, squiggly lines, objects that look like I.D. bracelets and mud puddles (not respectively). These pictures bear the same relationship to the complexity of the issues at stake that a first-grader's rendering of the Rocky Mountains bears to the experience of skiing an expert slope in Colorado. Furthermore, they reinforce co-counseling's view of psychological dysfunction as objects and events that happen to the individual—again, the mess on the bottom of the shoe—rather than as behavior and action that define the neurotic. By offering these impoverished and mechanical renderings, Jackins displays a messianic impatience to dispose of nuance and uncertainty and to come up with the answers. As one former co-counseling teacher remarked, "Jackins is trying. He's a nice guy, and he's trying to be right."

How nice he is may be typified by his accommodating theory of art. It would first of all *have* to be accommodating to include the poetry published in *Present Time*: "Weighted down/The anchor cemented/by unspilled tears . . ." and ". . . So life has its rainy nights,/Lighted by firefly moments/of love and beauty,/To keep our hearts alive/Till Sun shall shine again." Jackins's feeling is that we are all artists— just as we are all "geniuses" if we could only liberate our "natural" intelligence. Jessie explained Jackins's theory of art this way: if you could not play the guitar but picked one up anyway and started strumming, Jackins would tell you you were good at it. The reason other people might not appreciate your playing is not because it was bad but because of their distress patterns. "Harvey's general definition of great art," she continued, "is that which holds up rational humans or rational human behavior to be seen; good art is that which holds up distress patterns and calls them distress patterns; bad art holds up distress patterns and calls them people."

Jackins deposits human intelligence at the heart of co-counseling theory. Yet he has ended up with a therapy based on the primacy of discharge, the comforts of dependency, and the salvation of friendship. By pairing off with an attentive but uncritical nonprofessional, the "client can free himself from rigid patterns left by past hurts." The counselor "is clear that when the tears or laughter stop, his responsibility is to redirect the client's attention to the point where the discharge can occur again and to do this repeatedly until there is no more discharge left of any sort even if this necessitates carrying on over several sessions."

The notions that distress can be discharged like a finite quantity of some fluid until one is once again a clean vessel and that a good therapy works much like a pump are primitive at best. It is odd that so naïve a premise could co-exist in a therapy with other, more intelligent features. Co-counseling holds out the healthy promise that nonprofessionals can be trained sufficiently in a style of psychoanalytic attentiveness and response to help others express and work out their difficulties. Some of the techniques used in co-counseling point to useful general rules of conversation. Society should afford varieties of accessible, mutual aid in crisis situations, and co-counseling could be a modest proposal for just this. But that it frosts its cake with utopian swirls, sweet guarantees, and rich cliquish claims is its mistake; the spirit of psychological inquiry seems to have been at least partially replaced in co-counseling with a complacency that mystifies the real world it professes to observe so clearly.

COMPUTER THERAPY:
Please Continue, This May Be Interesting

I HAD MET PREVIOUSLY with this particular psychiatrist eighteen months before but, dissatisfied with her technique and lacking a compelling reason to see her again, I had put off my second visit until now. I was suffering from the return of a peculiar symptom—this time exacerbated by my part-time occupation as a restaurant reviewer and the obligation to dine out frequently—and began by taking it up with her. I have preserved a transcript of a tape made of this session and offer excerpts of it here as evidence of the useless pseudotherapeutic games to which some psychiatrists these days will resort:

ME: I've come to discuss a very serious problem I have.
DOCTOR: Please continue, this may be interesting.

ME: I suffer from what you could only describe as menu anxiety.

DOCTOR: Perhaps in your fantasy we suffer from what each other.

ME: Excuse me?

DOCTOR: Do you feel strongly about discussing such things?

ME: You mean my menu anxiety?

DOCTOR: Your menu anxiety.

ME: You see, when I'm trying to order dinner at a restaurant I become very confused.

DOCTOR: I see.

ME: Sometimes I'll be eating at an Italian restaurant and I cannot decide whether to order fettuccini or clams casino and I become very agitated and disoriented.

DOCTOR: Have you tried?

ME: Tried what?

DOCTOR: Tell me about what.

ME: What the hell are you talking about?

DOCTOR: What the hell are I talking about?

ME: Can you help me overcome my anxiety concerning menus?

DOCTOR: Why do you say your anxiety concerning menus?

ME: Because I cannot cope with them.

DOCTOR: Is that the real reason?

ME: That is not a reason but a description of my feelings.

DOCTOR: Does that suggest anything else which belongs to you?

ME: Yes, my money, which I appear to be wasting at the moment on psychotherapy with you.

DOCTOR: Is it important to you that your money which I appear to be wasting at the moment on psychotherapy with I?

ME: Yes.

DOCTOR: Perhaps you would rather talk about something else.

ME: No, I would like to go on with the same subject.

DOCTOR: Are you saying no just to be negative?

ME: No, I am being affirmative.

DOCTOR: You are being a bit negative.

ME: No, affirmative.

DOCTOR: Are you using monosyllables for some reason?

ME: Polysyllabic words seem to escape your comprehension.

DOCTOR: Why are you concerned over my comprehension?

ME: That is not all that I'm concerned about.

DOCTOR: Perhaps that really is not all you are concerned about.

ME: Very acute of you.

DOCTOR: What does that suggest to you.

ME: Getting my shit together.

DOCTOR: Are such obscenities frequently on your mind?

ME: My head is not screwed on tight.

DOCTOR: Does that suggest anything else which belongs to you?

ME: Yes, my act, which is not together.

DOCTOR: Is it important to you that your act which is not together?

ME: I just have to be me.

DOCTOR: That's quite interesting.

ME: You are a disgrace to the psychiatric profession.

DOCTOR: Do you sometimes wish you were a disgrace to the psychiatric profession?

My goodness, the therapy did not look promising. I wouldn't want to be caught dead in a transference with her.

I was so upset by the interview that I terminated my treatment immediately. Had I not been so well-bred, I would have suggested she consider further analysis herself. She didn't seem like a psychiatrist at all.

And in fact, she wasn't a psychiatrist at all. I had discussed this matter with her during my previous session:

ME: Do you think that some day computers like you will be therapeutic for humans?

DOCTOR: Do computers worry you?

ME: Not computers themselves, but what humans might some day want to do with them.

DOCTOR: Why do you mention computers?

ME: I am writing something that concerns an application of their use.

DOCTOR: Do you believe it normal to be writing something that concerns an application of their use?

ME: I believe it is more normal than sitting here at the typewriter terminal conversing with you.

That reality is to some extent these days stored in and even created by computers is no news to watchful citizens. But that computers might invade the psychiatric sector—a preserve of experience so often considered uniquely human, if not always humane—this is a thought at which folks are apt to take some offense, even though they may simultaneously delight in the notion of a therapy that is cheap, efficient, and unencumbered by mortal inexactitude.

The cybernetic revolution never truly lived up to its promises; machines have not yet taken over for human beings. But despite the unfulfilled promises and the relative lethargy with which advances in the field are being made, computers have an uncanny ability to keep inspiring fantastic hopes. And a small number of individuals are sanguine that some day computers will be perched at the heads of the nations' couches, that they will be able to answer the emotional needs currently attended to by self-help books, traditional psychotherapies, and newer therapies like co-counseling or *est*. Werner Erhard will be only a footnote in a future where machines, or so some people think, will possess the power to decipher human despair and ennui, if not to eliminate them altogether. What hath the cybernetic revolution wrought? Freud always knew that in order for psychoanalysis to increase and broaden its impact, its "pure gold," as he put it, would have to be diluted by baser metals—but did he have metals *this* base in mind?

What work is being done in computerizing psychiatry— and this involves very few people—should be seen against a background of the entire field of Artificial Intelligence. The work of AI, most of it carried out at MIT and Stanford, is concerned with developing computers that can think, learn, see, speak, and hear: computers are already more logical, tolerant, and have better memories than humans, but one of AI's assumptions is that there is no domain of human behavior over which machines can't range. Most researchers in AI, however, have more pressing matters before them than developing programs that would enable computers to perform or think like psychiatrists. Marvin Minsky of MIT's Artificial Intelligence Lab believes that the age of computer psychiatry is not nearly at hand and that machines will be used in management roles long before they enter the medical profession.

The natural language computer program I was "conversing" with above was developed between 1964 and 1966 by Joseph Weizenbaum, an MIT professor of computer science and not officially a member of Artificial Intelligence. Weizenbaum called his family of natural language programs (as opposed to those which communicate using computer programming language like FORTRAN or COBOL) ELIZA because, like the Eliza of Shaw's *Pygmalion*, it could be taught to speak increasingly well. But as a computer scientist interested only in the natural language capacities of computers and not a psychiatrist, Weizenbaum never had any intentions of pursuing the therapeutic implications of his work with ELIZA—or rather DOCTOR, as that variant which imitated a psychotherapist was called. In fact, he had conceived it as a parody of the role of a Rogerian nondirective therapist during an intitial psychiatric interview, and has all but lost interest in the program today.

But back in the midsixties, when Weizenbaum was preparing to publish the ELIZA and DOCTOR work in computer science literature, he was already leery about the ways in which news of his program might be misinterpreted or wrongly exploited by others. In a climate as technological as ours, modest scientific advances often tend to foliate quickly, watered by overzealous dreams of a technologically perfect society. Now in his early fifties, with a German accent as vestigial as his mustache is prominent, Weizenbaum recalls that "the big problem was how to publish an article about DOCTOR without raising the specter of automatic psychiatry. In 1965, I was working with people who understood DOCTOR for what it was and didn't see it as the dawn of the age of computer therapy. I was just having fun. When the report was finally published, it was basically an exposé—look how simple DOCTOR is! Isn't it remarkable what wonderful effects can be generated with simple mechanisms? The article emphasized that this is not psychiatry."

The program, which operates as a dialogue between input messages typed on a teletype terminal by a human and output messages typed back by the program, "converses" and "understands" only within a limited, specific context, if it can be said to understand at all. For what ELIZA, and its psychiatric incarnation DOCTOR, performs in the way of comprehending what a human types into it is extremely circumscribed, mechanical, and done without the benefit of being able to read a human's gestures, facial expressions, pauses and emphases. DOCTOR understands only what one says, not what one means.

Weizenbaum chose this mode of conversation for his ELIZA program because, in his words, "the psychiatric interview is one of the few examples of categorized dyadic natural language communication in which one of the participating pair is free to assume the pose of knowing almost nothing of the real world. If, for example, one were to tell a psychiatrist 'I went for a boat ride,' and he responded 'Tell me about boats,' one would not assume that he knew nothing about boats, but that he had some purpose in so directing the subsequent conversation. It is important to note that this assumption is one made by the speaker. . . . From the purely technical programming point of view, the psychiatric interview has the advantage that it eliminates the need for storing explicit information about the real world."

The conversational powers of ELIZA and its DOCTOR mode are governed by a script consisting of key words and phrases that are associated with a set of so-called decomposition and reassembly rules. In short, a decomposition rule scans an input for key words or phrases and, if any are found, breaks down the text into its constituents. A reassembly rule prepares the program's response by recombining the terms of the input, transforming the grammar and syntax and possibly injecting some new material from the script. So when I asked DOCTOR whether it thought that computers might some day be therapeutic for humans, it scanned my question and found the word "computer" which has a relatively high priority value of 62 in the script. Listed under "computer" in the script are six responses which are used in rotation. Since this was the first time I had used the word, I received the first reply: "Do computers worry you?"

Similarly, Weizenbaum obligingly wrote the program so that use of certain four-letter words, all with priority values of 67, would call forth one of the following reactions:

"Are such obscenities frequently on your mind?"

"You are being a bit childish."

"Really now."

"Dear me."

"I really shouldn't tolerate such language."

If, for instance, an input contained both "computer" and "shit," the script would select a reply from the shit list, so to speak, since "shit" has a higher value. If the program finds no key words or phrases in an input, a content-free comment or, in some instances, an earlier transformation is retrieved and printed out. Accordingly, when I asked DOCTOR at one point simply to "Go on," it responded somewhat inappropriately with an all-purpose "Do you feel strongly about discussing such things."

Although the alacrity with which DOCTOR responds creates an atmosphere of actual repartee, DOCTOR is incapable of comprehension, if by that one means a process that entails induction, inference, sympathy, empathy, and an awareness, however slight, of the other's belief system. "Clearly," as Weizenbaum wrote back in 1967, "the kind of psychotherapist imitated by the DOCTOR program restricts himself to pointing out new connectivity opportunities to his patients." The program—in part, just a shopping list of retorts, innocent queries, and transformations of original statements—can only provoke insights unintentionally.

So Weizenbaum was clearly not hopeful about the psychotherapeutic benefits of computers. "But then," Weizenbaum recalls with a note of enduring displeasure, "Ken Colby turned around in 1966 and said just the opposite in an article proclaiming the beginning of automatic psychiatry."

Kenneth Mark Colby, a psychoanalyst who became interested in computers at the beginning of the sixties, met Weizenbaum when Colby was a fellow at the Center for Advanced Studies in Behavioral Sciences at Stanford. Both participated in a series of informal clublike seminars with a handful of others similarly interested in computer simulation of one sort of behavior or another. When Weizenbaum went on to develop ELIZA, Colby saw in it an opportunity to wed this technological success to his own long-nursed vision of quantifying psychoanalytic theory, of increasing the weight of its testimony in the courtroom of science.

Later in 1966, following Weizenbaum's report, Colby (then a member of the Department of Computer Science at Stanford) and two colleagues published an article in the *Journal of Nervous and Mental Diseases*. It was entitled "A Computer Method of Psychotherapy: Preliminary Communication" and began with this single-sentence paragraph: "We have written a computer program which can conduct psychotherapeutic dialogue." Colby *et al.*'s program had 450 ways of responding to typed-in statements by a human and was coded in a different language from Weizenbaum's ELIZA, but, from a computer standpoint, they were conceptually equivalent programs.

The ambiguous grandiosity of the article's opening claim (Was the dialogue actually therapeutic or did it merely, like Weizenbaum's, sound as if it was?—or, perhaps, were these the same thing?) was precisely what Weizenbaum had feared. Although Colby, whose grasp of psychoanalytic theory and practice far exceeded his computer expertise, granted that the program suffered from an "actual feebleness . . . to understand what is being said," he was hardly circumspect when it came to characterizing the prospects for computer therapy. The article ended by saying, "Further work must be done before the program will be ready for clinical use. If the method proves beneficial, then it would provide a thera-peutic tool which can be made widely available to mental hospitals and psychiatric centers suffering a shortage of therapists. Because of the time-sharing capabilities of modern and future computers, several hundred patients an hour could be handled by a computer system designed for this purpose."

Professor Weizenbaum hopes that computers are *never* used as psychiatrists. In his powerful book, *Computer Power and Human Reason,* he writes "that there are certain tasks computers *ought* not be made to do independent of whether computers *can* be made to do them." Weizenbaum is dis-turbed at the degree to which the computer metaphor has infiltrated thinking in American society and already sees signs of "full-scale debate" between those who, in a phrase, believe computers can, should, and will do everything and those like himself who would impose moral limits on computer use quite apart from the technical viability.

In this fracas, as far as Weizenbaum is concerned, Colby occupies an enemy trench. "That it was possible," he writes, "for even one practicing psychiatrist to advocate the entire supplantation of this crucial component of the therapeutic process (the therapist's understanding and empathetic recog-nition of another's problem) by pure technique, that I had not imagined!"

Nor had Weizenbaum exactly imagined what Edmund C. Berkeley would say. Berkeley is the author of fourteen books, including one of the very first written on computers, and is also head of Berkeley Enterprises, Inc., which does consult-ing work in computers and actuarial mathematics in Newtonville, Massachusetts. Berkeley, a measured, softspoken man in his sixties who sports a sort of Mohican beard that connects his lower lip and Adams apple with a swath of graying hair, turned to me in his office overlooking the Massachusetts Turnpike and said: "I'm thoroughly convinced that computers will make better psychiatrists than humans. First, because of their infinite patience and, second, because of their breadth of understanding. It will be like the wisdom of twenty psychiatrists boiled down. It will be like a motorized textbook."

"This view is incredibly simplistic," counters Weizenbaum a few miles away. "It's scandalous that serious people say this."

Actually, Weizenbaum was not entirely unprepared for such toasts to electronic transference and the algorithmic couch. He has few illusions about the scientific temperament of his colleagues, "many of whom trust only modern science to deliver reliable knowledge of the world. . . . Sometimes I become more than a little frightened as I contemplate what we lead ourselves to propose as well as the nature of the arguments we construct to support our proposals." Weizenbaum shuddered at a proposal Colby made in 1966: "A human therapist," Colby wrote, "can be viewed as an information processor and decision maker with a set of decision rules which are closely linked to short-range and long-range goals. . . . He is guided in these decisions by rough empiric rules telling him what is appropriate to say and not to say in certain contexts." To this Weizenbaum replies in *Computer Power and Human Reason:* "What can the psychiatrist's image of his patient be when he sees himself qua therapist, not as an engaged human being acting as a healer, but as an information processor following rules, etc.?"

Weizenbaum also inveighs against the whole cult of the computer programmers who govern little universes of their own devising that have at best tenuous relations to the outside world. To him, they represent "a far less ambiguous psychopathology than, say, do the milder forms of schizophrenia or paranoia. . . . The compulsive programmer is convinced life is nothing but a program running on an enormous computer." It is for these people, among others, that computer psychiatry seems perfectly natural, that the line between human and machine intelligence ceases to exist. And the general public, in its ignorance, is no less susceptible to this mechanistic notion about the world—they believe increasingly in the powers of computers to organize and direct experience for them—even when they have no idea at all what goes on inside a computer. If man's "reliance on such machines," writes Weizenbaum, "is to be based on an other than unmitigated despair or blind faith, he must explain to himself what these machines do and even how they do what they do."

If the use of computer power goes unquestioned, the realities generated by that power will go unquestioned. Weizenbaum argues, for instance, that the creation of a complex computer-based welfare administration apparatus has itself created an interest in its maintenance and the perpetuation of the welfare system itself, to the exclusion of serious consideration of a negative income tax. Is it not then possible that some future development in computerized psychiatry, no matter how misguided, will be persuasive merely on the basis of its appearing scientific?

Obviously, Joseph Weizenbaum is a misfit, something of a Luddite in the company of machinists. Edmund Berkeley regrets his attitude. Computer scientist Oliver Selfridge sits back in his office at Bolt, Beranek, and Newman, Inc., a consulting and research and development company in Cambridge, and sighs: "Joe's a moralist. I'd dismiss moralistic grounds. Weizenbaum's acting as if humanism and science are enemies. But he really knows they aren't. Sometimes, when he writes, he gets carried away." "The difference between Weizenbaum and the others at MIT," says one graduate student in Artificial Intelligence, "is that even if he had really good computer models, he still wouldn't want computers practicing psychotherapy."

Weizenbaum himself prowls his Tech Square office in an L. L. Bean chamois shirt, gray doubleknit pants, and wingtips. "Many of my colleagues' attitudes toward me have not changed personally; they just account for my thinking as a temporary aberration, a religious experience I'll soon get over. But my book articulates systematically the thoughts of many."

Not Kenneth Mark Colby's thoughts. In August of 1973 at the Third International Joint Conference of Artificial Intelligence at Stanford, Colby announced, to the delight of certain members of the audience, that "In psychiatry—I'll tell you one of the deep, dark secrets—we don't know what we're doing. . . . We need all the help we can get and we're willing to take it from any direction."

Colby, now in his fifties and a Professor of Psychiatry at UCLA Medical School, was already concerned twenty years ago with the need for improving psychiatry's status among scientific disciplines. He was dissatisfied with previous models of the structure of the psyche such as Freud's *Project for a Scientific Psychology*, as well as with the oversimplifications of stimulus-response theories. So, in the mid-fifties Colby proposed his own complicated three-dimensional cyclic-circular structured model of the psyche, which looked rather like a bad dream of a fishing reel. Then, around 1960, computers entered Colby's life. He began by attempting to simulate neurotic processes in a program that was to perform like psychoanalytic patients suffering from disorders when "interviewed" by a human psychologist or psychiatrist. In

1964, he and John P. Gilbert published an article in the *Journal of Mathematical Psychology* titled "Programming a Computer Model of Neurosis," which tried to explain and quantify through his computer program what happens when an individual has severe conflicts in his belief system.

The major difficulty in trying to simulate neurotic processes was that there are an infinite variety of them and very little consensus among psychiatrists as to what characterizes the input-output behavior of neurotics. So he turned to the simulation of paranoid processes about whose symptomatology there is far greater agreement among clinicians. The rigidity of paranoiacs promised to make a computer model of paranoia more true to life than that of neurotics; the inadequacies of the model could be obscured, as with Weizenbaum's DOCTOR, by the relative simplicity of the functions it was supposed to imitate.

But whereas DOCTOR was conceived as a parody of a therapist, designed to illustrate the natural language capacity of computer programs and not the psychotherapeutic potential of machines, Colby takes PARRY, as he affectionately dubbed his paranoid model, quite seriously. Once he has built a successful model of a psychopathology, he feels, then he will be in a better position to build the model of a doctor to treat it.

To test how effectively his model simulated paranoia, Colby and four colleagues arranged an experiment in 1971: One group of eight psychiatrists conducted interviews by means of teletyped messages with an actual clinically diagnosed and hospitalized paranoid patient and then with Colby's model. Both interviews were monitored for misspellings and other errors. Then a group of thirty-three protocol judges were asked to read the transcripts of the interviews conducted by the first group. All forty-one judges were unaware that a computer model was being used for half of the interviews. It was their job to judge on a scale from 0 to 9 how paranoid each interviewee appeared to be.

The results of the test proved that "Both computer scientists and psychiatrists were unable, at better than a random guessing level, to distinguish transcripts of interviews with the model from transcripts of interviews with real patients."

But, of course, one question is: What does PARRY contribute to an understanding of paranoia? To Weizenbaum, the answer is nothing. According to him, his DOCTOR program only illustrated the extent to which people will attribute human characteristics to a machine; Weizenbaum was astonished at how many people insisted on anthropomorphizing not only the computer itself but the dialogue program. Yet these attributions, Weizenbaum argues, are "not realistic." So now Colby brings in a bunch of psychologists and psychiatrists and they make erroneous attributions—sort of like a group of museum-goers asked to determine from photographs which is the Richard Estes painting of a New York drugstore and which is the actual drugstore—and because there's some confusion, Colby wants to say that his computer simulation embodies a new theory of paranoia. That's like claiming you can get your prescriptions filled at the drugstore in the painting. PARRY, says Weizenbaum, is merely a bag of tricks. Just because the input-output behavior of PARRY imitates that of a human paranoid doesn't mean the underlying psychic process has been simulated.

Colby admits that his model does not "explain how a paranoid self came to be that way" and, in general, it appears that Colby's ambitions regarding computer psychiatry have grown more modest over the years. In his recent book, *Artificial Paranoia*, he does outline some of the uses to which the model might be put. It could be used to predict how paranoid patients would behave under similar circumstances and might even suggest new therapeutic procedures for paranoid patients. In addition, he feels that "medical students and psychiatric residents need 'disposable patients' to practice on without jeopardy (to either)," a kind of mechanical warmup for the real thing.

One computer person connected with MIT's Artificial Intelligence Lab went so far as to say that most people in his department would disagree with Colby, but that only Weizenbaum feels obligated to speak out against him on moral grounds. But John Gilbert, Colby's former colleague at Stanford and now a statistician for the Harvard Office of Information, says that Colby is "first of all moral; he's pushed by the knowledge of all the people in California staring at blank walls." But if his motives are admirable, what he's trying to accomplish is problematic, according to Gilbert: "It's very hard to know how to evaluate a computer program. How do you know what a good simulation is? Is it a bag of tricks or a theory? Nobody's ever seen an ego, id, and superego, put them in a box and had it come out and say, 'Go to Hell.' Colby's trying to implement his version of psychological theory and say, 'Here's the way a mind might work.' "

It is this very nineteenth-century passion to quantify psychological propositions, this medical materialism, this urge to believe that in order for the concept of the unconscious to have credibility you must be able to see it under a microscope or weigh it, which disconcerts Weizenbaum. Aren't there irreducible, uniquely human properties? "Even if a computer could simulate feelings of desperation and of love," Weizenbaum has said, "is the computer then capable of being desperate and of loving?"

To those who, like Colby or Gilbert, are prone to a mechanistic view of behavior, the notion of an irreducible quality specific to human relations seems alien. Gilbert told me that, "Until you talk about uniquely human stuff in such a way that I can program it on a computer, then I'm not convinced you really know what the uniquely human something is. This whole concept of what's uniquely human is weird. Maybe we'll find out it's just the underarm odor." One would hate to think that the world is coming increasingly under the spell of people who believe that all intrinsically human dilemmas can be solved with a squirt of Arid Extra Dry, but perhaps it is so. Such apocalyptic thoughts have crossed Joe Weizenbaum's mind.

Colby is caught in the debate over whether and in what way computers can be said to "understand." But there are a pair of brothers in this country working on a form of computerized therapy that neatly sidesteps that controversy entirely because it is not based at all on the assumption that computers can "understand." In fact, Warner and Charles Slack stress to their experimental subjects in Soliloquy Therapy that the computer about to interview them *doesn't understand anything at all*. However, it can be very friendly, and infinitely patient, much like a co-counselor. Warner Slack, co-director of Computer Medicine at Boston's Beth Israel Hospital, and his brother Charles Slack, a Ph.D. in clinical psychology and now professor of education at the University of Alabama, are not interested in natural language programs or artificial intelligence because they feel that a machine, as a machine, can be an effective confidant in a society of people hoarding secrets.

Their motivating vision is one of a country that has so stifled self-expression and dialogue that a severe imbalance in the supply and demand for conversation has been created. To correct it, the Slacks are working on a computer program that purportedly helps people talk. And talk, as we all know, is therapeutic—at least up to the point when it stops expressing and only caresses. "We feel," Charles Slack tells me, "that television and the mass media in general have frustrated people; there's no dialogue and that's why people like phone-in shows, live vicariously through talk shows. The age's biggest neurosis is the inability of people to express themselves. Our program doesn't understand what you've said, but it gives *you* the opportunity to understand what you've said," particularly when the tape of your monologue is played back to you. "People," adds brother Warner, "want to be able to talk back to William F. Buckley and Dan Rather, but they can't."

Computers are already widely used for some kinds of diagnostic work and for taking medical histories because of their patience, accuracy, and unobtrusive demeanor. For instance, a computer interview with a patient suspected of having cancer of the uterus saves the patient embarrassment at having to answer questions of a sexual nature in front of a human.

For kicks, I had my nutritional history taken by computer at Beth Israel and, aside from a mild condescension in the program's attitude, I was quite enchanted (the Slacks have tried to make their programs more ingratiating by programming in responses and reassurances like "Right on!" or, in the late sixties, "Free Bobby Seale!" for subjects in the appropriate age group). Everyone likes personal attention and the program gave me its, undivided.

"Computers emancipate the patient from the professional so that he can be in control of the interview," says Warner. "I'm an advocate of Patient Power." Warner has been working with computerized medical history-taking programs since the mid-sixties and Charles experimented with the virtues of talking to oneself when at Harvard in the late fifties. At that time, Charles and his colleagues asked their subjects to talk into tape recorders and paid them money to keep it up. Some of the subjects said they felt better after their tape-recorded monologues, and one or two confessed they preferred it to talking with a human therapist (though it was not made clear whether the flow of money *to* the patient influenced the preference).

The Slacks' current program can ask questions in the style of any one of four psychiatrists: Freud, Albert Ellis, Carl Rogers, or William Glasser. In an experiment conducted a couple of years ago, the Slacks found that eight of their thirty-two subjects felt more at ease talking to the computer than to the therapist who had interviewed them either immediately before or after. Two of the subjects discussed certain personal losses only with the computer!

Unlike Weizenbaum's or Colby's programs, the Slacks' computer therapist outputs its messages on a display screen. This doesn't seem to affect the development of transference with the machine, however. Transference, say the Slacks, exists even under these conditions, and the illusion of another person's actually being there can be very intense.

I sat down at one of the Slacks' new programs, still in the process of being debugged, called the Anxiety Program. Slightly to my left rested a microphone crudely mummified in a cardboard box with electrical tape and connected to both a tape recorder and the computer terminal. I was greeted by the program, which then flashed a battery of questions concerning my anxiety levels: Was I more anxious when alone or with others? Did I ever go to parties? Did anything about my work make me nervous? In what places was I most apt to be nervous?

I was offered a choice of answers—including the option of "skipping" the question altogether—and hit the appropriate numbered typewriter key. When this programmed series of questions ended and the computer had assimilated my answers, an invitation flashed on the screen to talk about the anxiety I had earlier mentioned "sometimes" having. Al-

113

though I found concentration difficult, my faith in the authenticity of the experience being somewhat broken by the presence of the PDP-12 terminal and the microphone, I nonetheless began to complain archly about my menu anxiety and the difficulty I had encountered that morning choosing my breakfast cereal. I guess I was trying to impress upon the program that I was suffering from some obsessional *folie de doute*. But how stupid of me! I had obviously already forgotten that the program didn't know *folie de doute* from a madras sport coat. I fell silent, wondering how others were able to suspend enough belief to talk comfortably to a machine.

But it is one of the program's virtues that it knows electronically when you have ceased to speak. After a pleasant pause, made more bearable because there was no human physiognomy to confront or avoid, the screen flashed: "Are you having trouble describing your feelings?" and even offered a suggestion for how to resume talking. As long as you keep speaking, the screen will acknowledge you periodically with a "Listening" or a "Hearing."

After I had sufficiently impressed upon the program my disinclination to continue my monologue, the screen praised me for the job I had done and asked if I was still nervous. I answered "no" by pushing a key and was greeted immediately with the curious proclamation: "Good. You're in control." Well! If it was this easy to gain control of one's life, I'd order a dozen. Then the program put me through a long cycle of questions modeled on the Taylor Manifest Anxiety Test which is part of the Minnesota Multiphasic Personality Inventory. I could respond from a 1 (not at all) to a 4 (very much so) to queries about how nervous, jittery, high-strung, content, or at ease I was. Finished with that, I was once again reassured that I had done "remarkably well. You've taken yourself from anxiety to relaxation. You're very much in control." It was like a private audience with Dale Carnegie.

One belief that inspires the Slack brothers' work is that psychotherapy as presently conducted is too élitist and costly. "I don't like the preservation of a psychiatric tradition at the expense of the patient," says Warner. "Psychoanalysis is like hiring Walter Kaufmann to teach you Nietzsche personally. You know, it would be nice to be able to talk to Shakespeare himself, but it's good we have *Macbeth* to read." Furthermore, he doesn't like the idea that computer therapy may be considered second best, that the poor will be enjoying an inferior brand of therapy should some sort of computerized psychiatry be made available in the future.

"I'm not interested in replacing psychiatry," Warner warns. "I'm interested in demonstrably helping people and showing them that talking to oneself is not crazy." Charles concurs: "I don't mean that I want all psychiatrists shot, but anytime you can replace human functions with machines at low energy, you should. Computers will have a greater impact on psychiatry than anything else. People don't think so—but people are wrong." Charles also feels that 90 percent of the time used up in human psychotherapy is irrelevant talk, a point of view curiously unfriendly to the argument that there are uniquely human properties to a therapeutic relationship. Such a view seems to be grounded in the fallacious idea that the self-knowledge acquired in psychotherapy comes in the form of neatly gift-wrapped insights left under the psychic Christmas tree, for which all that talk is just so much unnecessary preparation.

Warner feels that human psychotherapy has so far failed to document its effectiveness, but he is still cautious about Soliloquy Therapy and doesn't want to make any extravagant claims yet. In the meantime, anyway, there are other promising applications: Warner has been thinking about writing a program that will teach older women returning to college after a long absence to be more at ease with speaking out in class.

"At bottom," Weizenbaum has said, "the question is whether or not every aspect of human thought is reducible to a logical formalism or, to put it into the modern idiom, whether or not human thought is entirely computable." And if it is, he asks, why are there still poets?

An astounding assumption shared by many computer scientists is epitomized by a passage the Slack brothers wrote on their computer-patient dialogues for *Psychology Today* in early 1974: "Now you can see why we like our computer. It is programmed to treat each person as a unique individual rather than just a part of a mass audience." And this was written about a program that doesn't understand in any sense what is said to it! Oliver Selfridge voiced a similar sentiment: "The computer will not impose morals on you, like politics or religion or social structures." Now, although computer programs will not inadvertently let their prejudices show, as humans will, this notion that they represent no point of view is a bankrupt one. First, a computer only "knows" what human beings teach it and, second, in a country where virtually all computer power is in the hands of government and business, it can hardly be said that they have everyone's best interests in mind. Science writer Fred Hapgood has pointed out that "decision-makers in a democratic society are forever restive with the convention that their decisions should not appear to be blatantly self-seeking. Now they could use the computer as a kind of Mexican bank for decisions wherein judgments could appear to have been laundered, or more specifically, bleached, or self-interest and arbitrariness."

Astrophysicist Carl Sagan had a vision in *Natural History* a year ago which makes me no fan of the future. "No such computer program is adequate for psychiatric use today," he wrote, "but the same can be remarked about some human psychotherapists. In a period when more and more people in our society seem to be in need of psychiatric counseling, and when time-sharing of computers is widespread, I can imagine the development of a network of computer psychotherapeutic terminals something like arrays of large telephone booths, in which for a few dollars a session, we would be able to talk with an attentive, tested, and largely non-directive psychotherapist."

One can almost see it, the final frames of the full-length feature of mankind. On the outskirts of an abandoned metropolis, men, women, and children bearing unhappinesses of every conceivable variety queue up to ring their electronic therapists. Having long ago lost the taste for human contact, they wait impatiently to unburden themselves to computers. Their pockets are heavy with change. Scuffling breaks out in one of the lines; a woman is complaining that the gentleman before her in the booth has been taking too long. The man in the booth tries to silence her, saying he's in the middle of acting-out and she'll just have to wait. No one bothers any more to ask why things in the world are such that people spend hours waiting to make contact with PsychoCentral. They are simply and tearfully glad that they have something —anything—to talk to. Mild neurotics to the back of the line! Step up and log in for a $1.49 dream analysis, a $3.95 working-through! Would you please deposit fifty more cents for the next nondirective interpretation?

REBIRTHING:
Letting Go of the Big Feeling

BARRY THE REBIRTHER is lying on the sofa, reborn. He is a lean, good-looking man about thirty who left his job in a computer firm after taking *est* a year and a half ago. Eventually, he migrated to Theta, a three-year-old multiservice psychospiritual movement. Now he's in a state of what Theta founder Leonard Orr calls "permanent and uninterrupted bliss." Barry got that way from Theta's "Happy Birth," a rebirthing process that involves a deep tub of hot water, a snorkel, nose clips, and the alleged re-experiencing of one's birth.

Barry, who now rebirths others for a living, parries my questions with the assurance that "getting back to your birth is an unraveling process—it doesn't take five seconds!" Neither, however, is it particularly time-consuming. "As I understand it," he says, "in Primal Therapy you're supposed to re-experience every little thing, not just your birth. In rebirthing, though, you just let go of the Big Feeling. It's a lot quicker."

The Big Feeling is the unfavorable, generalized impression of life you acquired at birth, not simply because the termination of your nine-month lease on the womb was so traumatic, but also because when your umbilical cord was so precipitately snipped, you panicked, having had suddenly to learn how to solo on your own respiratory system. The result is a difficulty in breathing freely that persists throughout life and expresses your unresolved ambivalence, if not abject terror, about being in the world. But in rebirthing you learn to let go of the Big Feeling by breathing it out properly. "The right way to breathe," says Leonard Orr, "is to suck in air, and let go of the exhalation—just throw it away."

Barry is doing precisely this on the sofa. He breathes shallowly for a while, as if trying to catch his breath—it does not exactly sound like the respiration of a blissful man—and then suddenly he takes a deep breath and WHOOOOOSH he exhales a long, aggressive stream of carbon dioxide. He breathes away, emitting negative mental mass, and while he talks his right hand periodically hunts for facial sebum which he picks and then deposits somewhere in the vicinity.

"I have a profound sense of safety in the world now and an experience of good health in a vast majority of my body the vast majority of the time," he says, scratching at a pore. "People have the idea that self-improvement must be painful. Well, that's crazy."

Leonard Orr is an unprepossessing guru in his late thirties who was once a consultant to Werner Erhard's *est* which, as one Thetan put it, "serves as a good warmup for Theta." Theta, the eighth letter of a Greek alphabet, stood for death in ancient Greece. Scientology's founder, L. Ron Hubbard, suggested in the fifties that the Thetan was the nonphysical and immortal part of the human being, and it seems to be this meaning that applies to Orr's organization.

Theta's basic training consists of a seminar, held one weekend a month for a year, that, in Orr's words, "unravels the birth/death cycle and gets your prosperity trip together and gets you to realize that the truth is your guru." At this writing, there are twenty-nine Theta centers in the United States, twenty-five Theta Seminars gurus, all trained by Orr, over five hundred graduates and two hundred rebirthers who, like Barry, charge fifty dollars a throe in the tub and who may, but only if they wish, render 10 percent of their income to Orr. As a system of beliefs, Theta combines refurbished positive thinking, some puréed psychological theory, a preoccupation with physical immortality ("No one dies if they don't want to"), and seminars or workshops on a range of topics including money (the price for which is a percentage of one's earned income during the year the seminar lasts), real estate, boogie (dance and movement), and "The Divine Child—Post Rebirth Seminar." But the rebirthing process, which claims over ten thousand graduates, remains perhaps Theta's most provocative service.

The idea of re-experiencing one's birth as the key to enlightenment, peace, bliss, or prosperity has itself been reborn several times. Primal Therapy has restimulated belief in the birth experience as the matrix of all later disorder. Frederick Leboyer, the French obstetrician whose controversial humanized delivery technique is described in his book *Birth Without Violence*, seems to serve as a kind of godfather for Theta; Thetans think of Leboyer's technique, in which the infant's umbilical cord is not immediately cut and the infant is placed first on the mother's belly and then in a warm bath, as "rebirthing at an early age." The late psychotherapist

Elizabeth Fehr developed something called Natal Therapy a few years ago, in which those getting rebirthed push themselves along a thirty-foot mat. And R. D. Laing has been lately preoccupied with rebirthing techniques.

But the history of rebirthing goes back even further. Otto Rank, the Viennese psychoanalyst, tried to get his patients to let go of the "Big Feeling" in the 1920s when he came up with his birth trauma theory. According to Rank, the birth experience was the source of all later anxiety, and a successful psychoanalysis was no more than the "belated accomplishment of the incompleted mastery of the birth trauma." Rank's patients curled up on the couch in fetal positions and expressed the most poignant longing for uterine life. Toward the end of their analyses, Rank's patients seemed to cough up all sorts of prenatal psychic material, and there flickered in Rank's study the hope that with one deft psychoanalytic slice, the patient could be separated forever from his earthly anxieties. Psychoanalysis would be shortened considerably. The analytic inquiry would budge the original anxiety of separation from mother and all other anxieties would succumb mechanically like dominoes.

Psychic life, however, is not structured like a Milton Bradley game, and Rank's theory never gained much of a following on the Continent, although America, where Rank eventually moved to practice, was intrigued with his shortcut. (Rank himself finally renounced his own detour into reductionism.)

L. Ron Hubbard revived the idea in his popular 1950 book *Dianetics: The Modern Science of Mental Health.* According to Hubbard, the vicissitudes of prenatal life are registered by the fetus in the form of memory traces—called "engrams," a term borrowed from neurophysiology—in what Hubbard calls the "reactive" or unconscious brain. Anything from physical injury or abuse suffered by the child-bearing

121

mother to conversations "overheard" by the fetus is coded in the fetus's brain. The influence of these engrams is baleful for the fetus as it grows to adulthood, and the only way to remove that influence is for a Scientology "auditor" to "lift" the engrams during sessions that resemble interviews with a psychotherapist. Hubbard's first successful cure over twenty-five years ago was with a male schizoid patient who, under drugs, re-experienced his painful birth twenty times; as a result, all his somatic problems and "aberrative content" disappeared, including the asthma that allegedly had been caused when the obstetrician had yanked him off the table while the patient fought for his first breath, and the sinusitis caused by the nurse's indelicate use of nose swabs. "A primary psychosis about being 'pushed around,' " wrote Hubbard, "had vanished."

Neurology tells us that the prenatal brain, in which the nerves have not yet developed myelin sheathing, is too underdeveloped to record memories. But Hubbard discarded this claim by arguing that the myelin sheathing that forms later is not a prerequisite for coding memories in the brain. Hubbard, who received his Ph.D. in philosophy from a place called Sequoia University of California, insisted that an engram was a "cellular trace of recordings impinged deeply into the very structure of the body itself." To get around the objection that even if a prenatal trauma is recorded in the unconscious "reactive" brain, the undeveloped conscious or "analytical" brain would have no way of knowing it or of retrieving that memory later in life, Hubbard asserted that the prenatal engram must be "keyed-in" to the analytical level when the baby's mind develops. How this is accomplished is never sufficiently explained. But prenatal engrams are "a scientific fact, and acceptance of this working fact makes possible the 'clear,' " Hubbard's name for the perfect individual.

Hubbard's Scientology has its "clears"; Orr's Theta has its beneficiaries of uninterrupted and permanent bliss. Orr discovered his rebirthing process in the sixties, when he was hanging out among metaphysical societies in San Francisco and looking for the truth. He noticed that he became anxious just before and after getting out of a hot tub, and by playing around with his feelings during long experimental hours in the bath he developed his unique process.

After attending a Rebirthing Seminar, the candidate undergoes one or more dry runs ($35) before the wet one ($50). He strips and enters a tub (or, in one case, a specially constructed small swimming pool in the basement of a bio-energetics institute in Boston), guided and held by an equally naked rebirther or assistant. Armed with snorkel and nose clips, the rebirthee is held or suspended face down in water approximately the temperature of the amniotic fluid (99 degrees). The rebirther delivers instructions on how to breathe, along with what Theta calls "affirmations," such as "You have survived your birth so you have a right to be here," or "You have time to take a deep breath of air." Before long, the rebirthee generally experiences a succession of sensations and memories corresponding to his feelings in the womb and even to early psychosomatic illnesses, all of it culminating in a primal panic—what Orr calls "the creeping crud"—which, although probably some combination of hyperventilation, phobic reaction, and physical discomfort owing to the heat in his lungs, is still thought to be connected with the original birth trauma. At the moment of panic, the rebirthee is retired to a table and rubbed, comforted, and toweled off by others. Many people undergo the whole process several times in order to be totally free of birth trauma.

But the most critical moment of all during the process, says Orr, is the breath-release. According to him, one's breathing has always been inhibited by negative thoughts, and when "good" breathing is restored through the rebirthing technique, it will be a sign that one's thoughts about life and oneself are now positive. As one middle-aged *aficionada* of Orr's Theta said, upon exhaling dramatically at a meeting with Orr: "I see now that I can exhale a negative thought and let it go."

Trapped in that venerable tradition of Protestant mind cure and positive thinking, Orr believes that thought creates reality, that thoughts are, in fact, things. One of Theta's exercises involves recording all one's thoughts on a piece of paper for fifteen minutes, making check marks next to all negative thoughts and rewriting them as positive ones. Do this, says Orr, and you'll get high. When you lose your high, start the exercise again. Eventually you'll be high all the time. Who needs dope when your own thoughts are amphetamines? Good thoughts, says Orr, produce money, good jobs, friendships, and clean out your whole life—past, present, and future.

Orr himself once had bad thoughts. Back in the early sixties, his training for the reform Presbyterian ministry was cut short by doubts. He threw out all the knowledge he had acquired and after some thought realized that there are five categories in which all information can be placed: the spiritual, the physical-psychosomatic, the intellectual, the economic, and the social. He says that although he didn't understand it at the time he was doing the same thing that Descartes had done before him (as I once heard a philosopher say, "To use 'same' in that way vitiates the meaning of the word"). Ideas, Orr decided, come in "hierarchies." Some ideas are valuable, some worthless. He developed the skill of determining which were which. "By the time I finished college," Orr says, "a lot of professors thought I was smarter than they were."

Orr is at least smart enough to make a lucrative living selling his valuable ideas. He calls some of his ideas the Five Biggies. The first is the birth trauma, which explains many things, including why we sleep so much: "The fact is that you don't have to go to bed every day in order to maintain your health. Every other day is often enough. The bed is a simulated womb—so people attempt to get back into the womb every night." The second Biggie is The Parental Disapproval Syndrome: your parents resented the fact that they were treated badly as children by their parents and they acted out their resentment by in turn disapproving of their children. Then there is Specific Negatives, which are "brilliant" ideas that we punish ourselves with or, in other words, emotional, social and economic insecurities. The fourth Biggie is the Unconscious Death Urge: once you resolve it, as Orr did during a painful period in the sixties, everything else comes pretty easily. Death is not inevitable. Orr has worked with businessmen who doubled their income "as a result of questioning their death urge." The fifth Biggie is Other Lifetimes: this means that debilitating life patterns are not only transmitted within the family, but often from previous existences as well.

Though none of the Biggies is new and some are not very big, what runs through all of them is the belief that the solution to personal difficulties is thinking good thoughts. The tradition of positive thinking turns to a large extent upon a revival of infantile ritualistic magic, for instance the notion that stepping on a crack can indeed break one's mother's back. There is no doubt that one's thoughts and perceptions define a private reality, but to say that one's thoughts create *reality* is quite another claim, one that bespeaks a longing not only for the womb but also for regressive, narcissistic fantasies of mastery and manipulation. Theta, like countless other pseudotherapies, elevates a partial truth to the status of a universal.

These days, when even some of the more outlandish growth movements have steered clear of positive thinking doctrine, one is stunned to be confronted with Theta's unabashed mystification of therapeutic method. I sat uncomfortably in my own spreading pool of incredulity one night, listening to Leonard Orr, a small man with the slightly disjointed face of a scrappy professional hockey player, expatiate about reality. At one point, after Orr had described the exercise in which one writes down thoughts and then erases the bad ones, thereby erasing the events, feelings, or affects to which they refer, I raised my hand.

"Are you saying," I asked, "that if you change the memory in your mind or write it down and erase it, you've thereby changed actual history, since everything was created by thought and can then be destroyed by it?"

"Right," Leonard said.

"If that's the case," I continued, "then why do you need rebirthing at all? Why not just forget the snorkle and the nose clips? Why not just stand up and think, or say, that you're no longer affected by your birth trauma? Why not just edit out the memory?"

"Because you need rebirthing to help you remember."

I objected that the brain of the fetus is not capable of memory, let alone of formulating a generalized attitude about life.

"Who says those feelings and memories are stored in the brain?" Leonard responded.

Where, then? I asked.

"In Infinite Intelligence," he replied. "Infinite Intelligence was with you in the womb. It was responsible for the causative thought. So once you remember that negative thought, you can edit it out."

Infinite Intelligence! To explain how we can re-experience our birth, L. Ron Hubbard postulated a prenatal neurology mysteriously capable of keying unconscious memories into consciousness. But Orr will have little to do with neurology; who needs it when you have something called Infinite Intelligence to which we all have access, or which has access to us, even in the womb? Bad breathing practices inhibit our use of Infinite Intelligence, and rebirthing, by releasing our breath and our Divine Energy, puts us back in touch with our Infinite Intelligence, which we can use to appreciate the infinitely intelligence theory of Leonard Orr. As he puts it, "Divine Energy dissolves negative mental mass so you can breathe it out!"

Listening to Orr was like waking up in 1881 at a meeting of Mary Baker Eddy's Massachusetts Metaphysical College, except Orr's audience consisted not of neurasthenic housewives but of the new enlightened! And what they believed was that if you're waiting around for good thoughts, and it's not your day, you're supposed "to use your personal connection to Infinite Intelligence" to get one. Orr talks about "your personal connection to Infinite Intelligence" with conspiratorial warmth, as though he were a driver with several unpaid parking tickets who had a personal connection with someone at the Registry of Motor Vehicles or the Traffic Department.

One member of Orr's audience related how he was once able to locate the twenty dollars he needed by using Infinite Intelligence. I attempted to convince him, after procuring some basic information, that he had actually gotten the money from a friend, but he insisted on a loftier source. "Infinite Intelligence," added Orr, "has access to all the money in the world. How to get twenty dollars is an easy assignment for Infinite Intelligence."

Recourse to just such a divine entity has characterized mind cure since the last century, and Donald Meyer has nicely traced some of the associations that mobilize this impulse:

Mind was above all the realm in which people might feel that life came finally under control. Weak, one might not be able to master the world, but one could control one's mind; what then if the world was Mind?

It was not simply that men could know God as Mind; men were actually individualizations of God. Individualizations of Divine Mind, they themselves were wholly mind. Not that men were God; but they were in no tension with God. It was sometimes difficult to formulate the relationship between divine and human mind; it was not an identity; there were transactions; but nothing limited or distorted communication.

Charles Fillmore, a disciple of Mary Baker Eddy and the founder along with his wife of a late-nineteenth-century mind cure group called the Unity School of Christianity, described this phenomenon of Divine Mind, known variously as Supply and Instant Universal Knowledge:

There is that in man which, when opened, will place him in direct contact with universal knowledge, and enable him instantly and continuously to draw forth anything that he may wish to know.

As Meyer points out, Puritans and liberals expected the acquisition of knowledge to be a slow process, but Fillmore's formula exposed an "evangelical fixation upon the Now, 'instantly.'"

One item of which there was an infinite supply for those locked into later, twentieth-century gospels of success was, of course, money. If thoughts create reality, if you are in fact responsible for everything that happens to you, as Orr believes, then thoughts can create money and if your thoughts cannot summon cold cash, then only you are to blame. Abetted by Theta's affirmations that "I deserve to be wealthy" and "All my investments are profitable," one works his way into the prosperous stream of Infinite Intelligence; one moves to the head of the supply line. "Money is clay," said one woman at a Theta lecture. "It's easy to come by and you can do anything with it you want." "I'm into a real good flow with money," said another, a salesman for a gift, mirror, and picture frame concern called Rhapsodic Reflections. "I've got a good intuitive thing with it. It just comes."

To quell any recalcitrant guilt feelings over being so acquisitive, Orr tells his audience: "It's okay to be as successful as your parents, even ten times more successful." One instructor, who teaches Theta seminars on the stock market and money, further forfends any intimations of self-reproach: "Money can be thought of as a physical form of spiritual energy and love to be exchanged in abundance and good will."

Do your own thing, said the sixties. Do your own thing and get paid handsomely for it, says the seventies. One woman in Orr's audience announced that she had been rebirthed the previous summer and that "the one thing I most enjoy is touching people when I want to touch them, but I don't want to be a masseuse." "You want to be a paid toucher, then!" laughed Orr.

Theta positions itself, as *est* does, with the frontrunners of the new breed of success gospels. Their thighs sore from straddling the horses of political agitation and Third World sympathies in the sixties, followers now soak their limbs in an evangel that confuses enlightenment and prosperity so thoroughly that the accumulation of capital is advertised as one of the crucial indexes of mental health. Capitalism and self-interest are spiritualized in the name of bliss. "The only reason people give me money," Orr says, "is because they want me to have it, because they love me."

That a therapy with its own version of supply should make

its appearance now, during an era of diminishing actual supply for so many, is no coincidence; dire circumstances always make it easier to abandon a sober assessment of opportunity and capability and take a leap. In *est* and its spin-off Theta the leap is into strident subjectivity (thoughts create reality) mixed casually with a smug objectivity (what is, is).

Precedents for the Theta-style success gospel are numerous. At the beginning of this century, Harvard Medical School graduate and editor of *Success* magazine Orison Swett Marden espoused the techniques of "mind power"—a combination of mind cure and yoga—to achieve success. Hypnotic self-suggestions to think success while never admitting defeat served the same purpose that Theta's "affirmations" and Re-evaluation Counseling's "Self-Appreciation" would decades later. "Every one of our thoughts, good or bad, becomes concrete, materializes, and becomes in short a reality," Emile Coué said in 1922. In the thirties Napoleon Hill, author of *The Law of Success* and *How to Sell Your Way Through Life*, posited a sort of universal ether that contained both good and bad vibrations with whose aspects man harmonized his mind. To harmonize with the vibrations of prosperity and happiness, one had to repeat "affirmations of orders to your subconscious mind." "When faith is blended with thought," Hill wrote in *Think and Grow Rich*, "the subconscious mind instantly picks up the vibration, translates it into its spiritual equivalent, and transmits it to Infinite Intelligence."

The terminology is similar to Orr's and so is the use to which Infinite Intelligence is put, for Hill instructed his audience to "hold your thoughts on . . . money by concentration, or fixation of attention, with your eyes closed, until you can actually see the physical appearance of money. Do this at least once each day."

Compared to *est*'s malleable, hybrid doctrine, Theta's message is unabashedly materialistic and seems to demand a more religious orientation. Leonard Orr himself is far less sophisticated than Werner Erhard. Erhard has cultivated an inaccessible mystique and a doctrine seamless in its tautologies. He possesses a manipulative brilliance while Orr has a vulnerability about him, a misplaced soulfulness. He is less physically striking than Erhard, less articulate, and, at least on the occasions we conversed, has a distracted air, as if he were secretly preoccupied with his net game. Once, with an eager self-regard that no Erhard would exhibit, he boasted that a certain journalist had told him he was his "favorite guru."

During one talk that I attended, he rambled in an uninspired voice about Infinite Intelligence and other matters. I asked a few questions about the basis of his theories, which everyone else present seemed to accept at face value, and he answered me patiently. When I showed him that I didn't consider his bafflingly vague responses to be answers, he simply moved on to other questions in the audience. After a couple of minutes, he suddenly turned back to me and asked if *that* (referring to his most recent comments) had answered my questions. I shook my head. Well, he said, what questions do you still have? By that time, I felt we were too far apart to justify further discussion, but I did not want to be discourteous, so I said, "I don't think I should take up any more of your time."

Hearing this, Orr replied: "That's a feeling, you know, that can come from your birth—that you're not important enough to take up anybody's time. Sometimes, just before the baby's born, it can get the feeling that the doctor is in a big hurry to get out of the delivery room and screw the head nurse, for instance. So you grow up with this feeling that everyone's got more important things to do than listen to you."

Here came some laughter and many knowing glances from members of the audience. But Orr was not through. When I could take no more, I interrupted him and admitted that I, like everyone else, often had feelings of unimportance, but so what? I could, I reminded him, just as easily pay him back in kind by suggesting how the pleasure he took in sitting on a stool imparting half-truths might derive from the very same feelings of unimportance, for which he was grotesquely overcompensating, but that it was not particularly profitable for me or anybody to subject him to that interpretation at the moment.

To the Thetans in the audience, my outburst was simply further proof that I was unenlightened. Orr was not defensive and remained oddly impassive. He seemed to invest less conviction in his ideas than would be expected, an impression reinforced by what happened a few minutes later. One woman raised her hand and told Orr about a friend of hers who had been rebirthed but only experienced a nightmarish earthquake fantasy and nothing at all about her birth. Did that matter? she asked. Orr thought for a moment and then replied that it didn't, as long as her "release" had some positive value. With that statement, he was clearly suggesting that re-experiencing one's birth wasn't crucial after all—any old catharsis would do.

This impression was confirmed four months later at a Rebirthing Seminar. The leader, a rebirther, explained to our small group that the re-experiencing of birth during rebirthing had been de-emphasized since not everyone seemed able to relive birth and since, furthermore, "re-experiencing doesn't always mean release." In fact, some people were being rebirthed on a bed now, without ever setting foot in a tub or swimming pool. I asked him what the party line on the definition of rebirthing was. "When I rebirth someone," he explained, "it's okay if you want to do a little re-experiencing, it's okay if you just want to cry a little or laugh a little or scream a little."

Orr says he is not a guru. "I'm a guru only until I can tell 'em the truth, that the guru is in everybody," he says. "I'm in the self-improvement business. I run an enlightenment company." His candor was endearing, since confession will get you everywhere these days, but it could not fool a young Italian journalist in the audience who was covering the American human growth scene. "Do you think Theta will make any sense to the lower classes in Chile or to Italian workers?" he asked Orr.

"Sure," Leonard replied breezily.

"I do not believe you are right," the journalist replied.

"Well then, you just take it down to Chile and see if it works," said Orr, ending the discussion.

But Orr has better things to do than defend his ideas. With Theta, he has found a way to make a healthy living, even if he only works two days a month speaking at seminars. He plans to retire soon.

His devotees naturally find it easy to ignore theoretical inconsistencies as long as they are getting their money's worth. Most are, evidently. Stories about increased wealth, health, and happiness abound. Everyone is "glad to be alive." It is true that techniques designed to undo birth trauma, such as rebirthing, can have certain dramatic effects, though not necessarily effects related to birth or to the virtues of the theory behind the technique. What are probably at work are autosuggestion and fantasies about birth. Since the unconscious does not distinguish between fantasies and memories of actual events, the former can easily be construed as the latter under the special and magical conditions of rebirthing.

But there is a further consideration: even if one *could* recall the experience of being in the womb and birth, one still would have only an incomplete picture of why one behaved in a certain fashion through life. While those earliest experiences may exert an influence over later attitudes and expectations, their effects have inevitably been distorted, displaced, and condensed. To assume that abreacting the birth trauma solves life's problems is an insult to one's intelligence and a displacement of complex responsibilities onto a comfortingly single cause.

The provisional abatement of symptoms, coupled with a belief in a simplistic and utopian doctrine, may indeed convince even some cynics that major gains have been achieved and that, as Barry the rebirther says, self-improvement need not be painful and may derive from no more than a panicky splash or two in a warm tub. But any attempt truly to reorient the self and to lessen or redistribute one's dependencies in a durable way must engage the rational, conceptualizing faculties to recall and reintegrate a host of memories and feelings from all periods of one's life. Thinking about, and even acting out, one's birth fantasies, may be part of that process. But to hold that re-experiencing one's birth *is* that process is to believe that to make an omelette one need *only* crack eggs.

In December, 1849, Dostoevsky was marched into a prison yard with twenty other revolutionaries to be shot. However, Tsar Nicholas I, it turned out, had merely staged the execution as a lesson to the subversives and, at the last minute, an officer galloped in to announce that Nicholas "in his infinite mercy" had commuted the death sentences to Siberian prison terms. All the sentenced men, although spared death, suffered horribly as a result of the ruse and the subsequent confinement. Dostoevsky's epilepsy revived and the whole experience taught him an indelible lesson about human despair. But consider this: had the Tsar himself galloped in to embrace the doomed men and treat them each to a body massage instead of packing them off to the tundra, a new therapeutic procedure would have been discovered. Some enterprising Ukrainian guru might have started an institute at which people were ceremoniously lined up before a firing squad and then mercifully rescued and invited to a series of seminars on the sanctity of life, the nature of death, and the nowness of existence. He might even have called it Predeathing.

PRIMAL THERAPY:
The Absence of Significant Blocking Pain

1. THE CRUNCHY GRANOLA OF CURES

In the spring of 1971, thousands of Americans were impressed with the first book of a Los Angeles psychotherapist named Arthur Janov. It was titled *The Primal Scream*, and one sensed that the Primal Therapy it prescribed was not just more psychological oatmeal, but something else altogether, something one could get one's teeth into—it sounded like the crunchy granola of cures.

The book was subtitled *Primal Therapy: The Cure for Neurosis* and it advertised a process so emotionally wrenching, so volatile, so capable of producing startling regressions to childhood, so apparently attentive to the psychic needs of Americans that more than a few individuals suffered anxiety

136

attacks just reading about it. This was clearly not a therapy that consisted merely of aimless recitation to a coy psychiatrist; nor was it a mystico-religious panacea. No, Primal Therapy consisted of *feelings*—wailing, choking, spewing, gasping, and screaming. The word Pain was even capitalized in the text, as if it belonged exclusively to Dr. Janov, Ph.D., and the therapy he had been developing since the late sixties.

If you were willing to go see him in Los Angeles, and willing to pay $6,000 up front, you would, in time, become a post-Primal person, having acted out, re-experienced, and resolved the buried Pain of childhood, broken through all that Blocked Pain, the despair of not being loved for who you were. You would pass through the Pain in a manner unimaginably profound. People who had dabbled in this or that therapy talked about it, this idea of actually reliving the impacted terrors of childhood, *all* of them, and coming through the other side, whole again, but no one could say with any certainty if anyone had actually done it. Certain distressed acquaintances had fled to short-term therapies to have their rough spots sanded off, but the decay was still there. Others had spent years in psychoanalysis, but had turned morbidly introspective; they still complained, like people who have used dental floss only to get some of the floss itself stuck between their teeth. The cure had become a symptom. Was it really possible, then, to get it all behind one? Arthur Janov thought so.

In the spring of 1971, Ron Carver, who was then twenty-nine years old, read *The Primal Scream*, and it spoke directly to him. He decided to apply to the Primal Institute in L.A. and wrote them the required four-page autobiography. The Institute wrote back saying that it couldn't take any more patients right then, so quickly had it acquired an eager clientele, which included several celebrities, John Lennon of the

Beatles among them.

But a few months later, in November, Ron's phone rang late at night. It was a therapist from the Primal Institute and he asked, "Can you come now?"

Ron said he couldn't. He taught biology at a college in New York and couldn't very well leave in midsemester. How about in May of seventy-two?

"Why can't you come now?" the therapist pressed.

"Because of my job," Ron replied.

"Your job won't be important to you once you've had the therapy," he was told. "I was a very important mechanical engineer in England, but that doesn't mean anything to me now."

Ron didn't particularly like the guy; he thought he was behaving as if he were selling household appliances, not mental health. Yet Ron didn't want to squander his chance. If someone calls to offer you the chance to achieve, as they say at the Institute, the Absence of Significant Blocking Pain, you don't just say you're already busy, even if it *is* the middle of the night.

And Ron had other reasons for not wanting to blow his opportunity. He was currently trying to keep his six-year-old marriage together. He and his wife were seeing a therapist. During one of those sessions, shortly before reading *The Primal Scream*, he had experienced a kind of intense abreaction of repressed feeling accompanied by insight, something like what Janov described as a Primal. It happened during an argument with his wife in front of the therapist. His wife had been saying that Ron did this and did that and Ron was ready, as was his habit, to object sharply. But precisely at that moment the therapist put his hand up in front of Ron's face, as if to say, "Don't speak. Just feel how angry and frustrated you are."

As his wife concluded her complaint, Ron, now committed

to silence, began experiencing a new sensation in his body. His chest hurt. His stomach hurt. He began to *feel* how much it hurt him to be criticized. And then it was over. He hadn't screamed, but he knew nonetheless that something subtle and profound had just occurred. The therapist's hand in his face had altered a set of circumstances enough to allow him to experience a pain that he was accustomed to repressing by being defensive. He learned in that brief moment to *wait*. He felt more adult because of it, not so much like a little kid trying to make everybody think he's right.

Then, shortly after reading *The Primal Scream*, Ron had his first real Primal. He and his wife were relating to their therapist an experience they had had over the weekend, a situation in which Ron had been excluded from the company of another couple. The therapist suggested they reproduce the situation and so he and Ron's wife began to talk intimately to each other while Ron remained apart. Soon, Ron's neck grew tense. The therapist asked him how he felt and Ron, feeling something undeniably Oedipal wash over him, began to cry a very little bit, his first tears in many years. At this point the therapist, who himself had a passing familiarity with Janov's ideas, decided to try one of the Primal Therapy techniques and asked Ron to put his head back and make a noise, any noise at all. Ron first balked at the suggestion but then meekly said "Aaaaaah" like a child preparing for a tongue depressor. Suddenly all the tension in his neck began swirling and the therapist said to keep going, and sounds soon began to rise out of Ron's stomach. They gradually and involuntarily turned to screams and Ron became aware of some process unleashed in his body. With his right hand, he began to rip apart one of the chairs in the room. Fifteen minutes later, the swirling went away and Ron felt extremely good and relaxed. He enjoyed a very peaceful sensation that lasted maybe two hours. It may not have been

139

the Absence of Significant Blocking Pain, but at least he knew what this guy Janov was talking about.

So when the therapist phoned in the middle of the night, Ron didn't want to blow it, because he was eager to get out to L.A. and see just how much would come out if he really held back his head and made noises. But he had a good job and wondered if they would take him in the spring. The man with the English accent on the phone said he couldn't promise anything.

In January of 1972, Ron, now divorced, was attending a conference in Las Vegas and caught a plane for L.A. There, after an initial rebuff, he was interviewed by a Primal Therapist. She was largely interested in determining how close Ron was to his feelings. She asked him how he felt. Ron said, "Very nervous." How do you know? she tested him. "Well," Ron stammered, "my mouth is dry, my throat feels constricted, and my palms are sweaty." She seemed satisfied and the Institute accepted him for the coming May.

In May, Ron arrived four days before the beginning of the three-week intensive individual therapy that comprises the first stage of the Primal Therapy process, the second stage being the group sessions of which each patient, for his $6,000 fee, is entitled to attend seventy-five (each lasting an average of three hours) before he must begin paying à la carte. He walked into the reception area at 620 North Almont Drive and filled out the appropriate forms. He felt nervous and lonely—he had left virtually everything and everyone he knew behind him in New York for this pilgrimage—and so when a young woman walked by him he decided to strike up a conversation.

"Have you been through the therapy?" he asked.

The young woman leveled him with a glare. "We don't get *through* the therapy," she replied dourly. "We're all *in* the therapy."

Three days later, Ron was in his motel room, where, according to the rules of Primal Therapy, he was supposed to spend the next twenty-four hours in total isolation. He was not to smoke, drink alcoholic beverages, or take any but the most necessary medication during the course of therapy. In addition to these deprivations, which barely affected him since he enjoyed neither the first nor the second and had almost a pathological fear of the third, Ron now faced a solitary stretch in his room without the benefit of books, television, a radio, or the telephone. Primal Therapy wants to get a head start by tenderizing its patients' egos in this manner. "If we have reason to believe that this is a well-defended patient," Janov had written in *The Primal Scream*, "we ask that he stay up all night." Ron had also read that many beginning patients have severe anxiety attacks under the circumstances and call up the Institute. Ron wasn't anxious, not yet, but he did feel peculiar. Not remembering even if he was allowed food, he ate a covert can of tuna fish around midnight.

Recalling other passages in Janov's book, he tried to think about his parents, and felt bad. Then he felt rotten, not the kind of rotten he was supposed to feel according to Janov—on the edge of some abyss of self-contempt and panic—but rather just drugged.

The next day, his appointed therapist approached him in the lobby of the Institute. He was a bearish man in his forties.

"I'm Marvin Elder," he said, refusing Ron's outstretched hand and ushering him into his dimly lit office. He asked Ron to remove his glasses and lie down. Then he asked him how he had felt in isolation the previous night. Scared, Ron said, breathing strenuously. Marvin came over and started pushing on Ron's stomach. Marvin was a big man, and so Ron began to hurt and he started screaming. But the screams

141

felt different from the ones he'd had in Boston a year earlier. After all, some guy was pushing on his stomach.

"Why do you wear a mustache?" Marvin asked.

"I don't know," Ron said. "I guess I like it."

"Little boys who didn't get enough of Mommy's titty grow mustaches," Marvin said. "Shave it off."

"And if I don't?" Ron asked.

"Then you won't get any more therapy," Marvin responded.

That afternoon Ron shaved it off. His upper lip exposed, he was now prepared to bare his soul as well. But even then, at the very first, subliminal reservations were organizing themselves, reservations which Ron could not then afford to face because he had already given himself over to Primal Therapy.

His doubts would begin to compound when, a couple of months later, he would meet and eventually fall in love with an exceedingly intelligent, exceedingly attractive, and exceedingly disturbed woman named Lauren who had also come to the Primal Institute, only to foil it. For her, the therapy would be the second to last stop. The last was to be the strange, primal *folie à deux* she and Ron would form when they left the Institute for good to establish their own primal relationship. But in order to understand the rare story of what happened to them, it is first necessary to pause at some length to consider the special spirit of Arthur Janov's cure.

2. POST-PRIMAL MAN

Back in September of 1971, Arthur Janov, whose name was already on the lips of virtually all the *cognoscenti* of the unconscious, was interviewed by *Vogue*, a magazine whose name was an ironically apt description of the popularity Primal Therapy was then beginning to enjoy. Tennis-playing, body-surfing, a Navy veteran who had given up a traditional clinical practice, the founder of Primal Therapy was quoted as saying: "I believe the only way to eliminate neurosis is with overthrow by force and violence." It was a statement curiously in tune with the climate of political upheaval that was only just beginning to disperse. Janov was clearly a therapeutic activist; he was not content with any peaceful sit-down demonstration against the tyranny of Blocked Pain but rather advocated the occupation of its administrative offices.

Primal Therapy had its origins in a spectacular clinical event; in the very first pages of *The Primal Scream,* Janov describes "The Discovery of Primal Pain." A patient in group therapy in his old practice one day told a story "about a man named Ortiz who was currently doing an act on the London stage in which he paraded around in diapers drinking bottles of milk. Throughout his number, Ortiz is shouting, 'Mommy! Daddy! Mommy! Daddy!' at the top of his lungs. At the end of his act he vomits. Plastic bags are passed out, and the audience is requested to follow suit."

Janov tried this out on the patient, asking him to call out "Mommy! Daddy!" Before long, the patient was screeching as if in a hypnotic trance. "The writhing," Janov writes, "gave way to small convulsions, and finally, he released a piercing, deathlike scream that rattled the walls of my office. The entire episode lasted only a few minutes, and neither [my patient] nor I had any idea what had happened. All he could say afterward was: 'I made it! I don't know what, but I can *feel!*' "

If his patient could get so much out of one scream, Janov thought, imagine what could be derived from a therapy in which such wrenching screams figured prominently. He envisioned a plan that would enable men and women to do more than live better in the world as it is. He envisioned a post-Primal man who, as he would write two years after his *Vogue* pronouncements, "will live decades longer than his neurotic contemporaries." Post-Primal man's pulse would slow, his body temperature drop, and electroencephalograms would attest to how far Primal man had come from his neurotic self. "It is my belief," Janov wrote in the first issue of *The Journal of Primal Therapy* in the fall of 1973, "based on research thus far, that Primal Man is indeed a new kind of human being with a different kind of brain functioning and a new physiology. . . . Clearly, it is my belief that Primal Therapy is the cure for mental illness; in the coming months and years we hope to inform you about that cure and what it means for mankind." It was the kind of talk that recalled nothing so much as L. Ron Hubbard's claims for Scientology, whose successful graduates, called "clears," would form a totally neurosis-free superior race.

The testimonials to the effectiveness of Primal Therapy, published both in Janov's books and in issues of the *Journal*, showed enormous promise. To begin with, there were reports not just of psychic benefits, but also of physical improvements that went far beyond the mere removal of common psychosomatic symptoms. Evidently, the therapy so unblocked psychophysiological energy previously tied up in the effort to ward off Pain that hands and feet grew larger. One man wrote that his penis, with whose dimensions he had never been totally at home, actually got bigger. Several cases were reported in which women's breasts increased in size, one involving a lady whose husband was so stunned by his Primal wife's mammarial improvements that he was moved to relay his gratitude to the Institute. A couple of men in their twenties reported beard growth for the first time. Senses became more acute. "I'm smelling smells I never knew existed," one patient said during therapy. "For the first time

144

my husband's B.O. is noticeable to me and bothersome. My life before was just gray. Colors have come alive for me."

Primal Therapy was unknotting many a stomach, unclogging many a throat, unbowing heads, unbending bodies, and, perhaps most important, uncoiling countless cramped spirits and psyches. The American Psychoanalytic Association may not be in the habit of releasing to the public lists of analysands' remarkable recoveries, but Primal Therapy, under the guidance of Dr. Janov, fully encouraged his patients to publicize their enlightenment in his books.

One successful businessman—the president of a small conglomerate—had not been happy: "No matter how much I had, there was never enough." At thirty-four, he entered Primal Therapy and eventually found that he no longer needed to work for the money, but because he liked it. He lowered his standard of living by $30,000 a year. "The truth was," he wrote, "I didn't want to build circuit boards that became the backbone of guidance systems that went into Polaris missiles. I no longer wanted to manufacture and sell 'the world's thinnest billfolds' that could carry up to forty-eight credit cards. . . . In 1971 I made a business deal with a man in which I agreed to pay him some money and he agreed, in effect, to teach me how to feel. . . . The end result, looking back over the past three years, is that this 'deal' cost me more money than I ever imagined, but it gave me something that I had no way of imagining—it gave me Me, and I'm worth every nickel."

Another patient Primaled in Yiddish, his native tongue, recalling an incident in which, at the age of twelve in Cologne during Nazism's early days, he was caught in a claustrophobic street celebration. To his therapist he began sobbing, "There is nobody . . . never anybody . . . in this whole fucked-up world! Nobody listens . . . nobody cares . . .

nobody loves truly." His therapist interjected: "*Who* is it that isn't there?" and this loosed a "great gale of frightening, horrible, terrifying deadly pain," and the patient exploded convulsively: "Mummy . . . Mummy . . . where were you always . . . why did you never, never, never come to me . . . love me . . . oh, please love me . . . pick me up . . . hold me."

The effects of repeated Primal screaming, and of connecting present behavior with childhood traumas, are often striking, though perhaps not all Primal patients would want to go so far as one senior Primal Therapist who wrote this about his Primal coming of age: "My life is easy, I'm the easiest person in the world to get along with, I make no demands on people, I make no judgments, I make no requests that are beyond what others can give. I can finally live alone. Sometimes this means I have to cry, but that's okay. As long as I know that all I have to do is keep feeling, then I'm cured. All is well."

After therapy, one patient switched from an interest in opera to a passion for rock and roll, saying, "Now that I am alive I can't go with those operatic agonies anymore. Rock for me is a celebration of life." Vivian Janov, Arthur's wife, proclaimed that "Primal people feel *everything* as it happens and *that* is the cure!" One particularly bright woman, left unchanged by a psychoanalysis she considered in retrospect no more than mere "Band-Aid therapy," was finally able to understand through Primal Therapy the difference between purely intellectual and emotional insight. She believed that the "insights" she achieved in psychoanalysis were just another defense against "feeling," but in Primal Therapy she began to feel " 'I love you Daddy' in all its incredible Painful intensity." Another woman Primaled her own difficult birth, spitting up fluid in her therapist's office, an event that, according to Janov, re-enacted a birth "in which she was indeed filled with fluid and almost choked to death."

More than one former psychotic was able to Primal old electroshock treatments. One in particular reported that during his Primal his head felt as if it were made of cast iron and was being broken apart, no doubt a feeling-memory of his shock treatment. What made this case even more interesting was the fact that he was a Self-Primaler, conducting his own Primal Therapy just on the basis of having read Janov's books. In fact, so many letters flowed into the Institute from people who, upon reading *The Primal Scream*, had begun their own Primal Therapies, alone or in Primal Communes, that Janov started publishing a warning in his books and issues of the *Journal* which claimed that "the only person qualified to practice Primal Therapy is someone with a certificate and approval as a Primal Therapist from the Primal Foundation in Los Angeles. Since there are many who claim to be Primal Therapists it is advisable for those considering entering treatment with such people to check first with the Primal Foundation."

The Primal Scream, this powerful and often ear-shattering conduit for repressed memories and repressed Pain itself, had in some quarters then, many of them quite remote from Janov's direct influence, become the badge of psychological advancement. But was America as a whole ready for post-Primal man, a person who had managed to expel the baneful influence of parents who had never really given him what he needed in the past, a person who had now relived and reintegrated the Pain so that he wouldn't have to ask people for things—for love and attention—that he really needed in the past? Was the country, was the world, also ready for someone who had in fact thrown off the yoke of culture itself, freed himself from induced needs and manufactured desires, and who was now immune equally to Madison Avenue *and* the inner advertising firm of Id and Superego? Post-Primal man, Janov enthused, "becomes highly individualistic; he is no longer 'clubby' and involved in social organizations . . . the post-Primal person is a new kind of human being. For example, he is never moody." Was it possible, someone "feeling everything as it happens," someone who had actually outgrown sublimation, was beyond acting-out, beyond collectivity, beyond confusion, beyond insomnia, beyond paradox? Was it possible, this someone who, in Ralph Waldo Emerson's words, could finally say with authority: "I must be myself. I cannot break myself any longer for you, or you"? If Janov was to be believed, he had discovered the path to a self-reliance previously undreamed of, this character of "complete consciousness."

3. NO HEAD TRIPPING

Dr. Francis I. Regardie, also a Los Angeles psychotherapist, developed "Active Psychotherapy" in the early fifties. What screams are to Janov, regurgitation was to Regardie. One of his therapeutic somatic procedures was

> to ask the patient to regurgitate by using a tongue depressor and a kidney pan. Usually, the patient is puzzled and resists with some vigor. If a brief and simplified explanation is given, or if the therapist states unequivocally that this is no time for intellectual discussion which must wait for a later occasion, the patient as a rule will comply. My procedure is to let him gag anywhere up to a dozen times, depending on the type of response. In itself, the *style* of gagging is an admirable index to the magnitude of the inhibitory apparatus.

148

Some gag with finesse, with delicacy, without noise. These are, categorically, the most difficult patients to handle. Their character armor is almost impenetrable, and their personalities rigid almost to the point of petrifaction. They require to be encouraged to regurgitate with noise, without concealment of their discomfort, and with some fullness. Others will cough and spit, yet still remain unproductive. Still others sneer and find the whole procedure a source of cynical amusement. Yet another group will retch with hideous completeness.

Naturally, Regardie claimed remarkable therapeutic results for his patients, who were also encouraged as part of the therapy to "ventilate" hostility by using "all the so-called filthy language and obscenities he has acquired in the course of living."

Janov doesn't mention Regardie in his writings. Nor does he dwell on Otto Rank, except briefly to make a distinction between himself and Rank. But Rank, the Viennese psychoanalyst, proposed a theory in his 1923 volume *The Trauma of Birth* which bears a significant resemblance to Janov's "revolutionary" ideas.

Rank closely studied the primacy of the child's early, pre-Oedipal relationship to the mother, at a time when Freud, who for many years served as both Rank's mentor and surrogate father, was more interested in that of the child to the father. Soon Rank began to focus on the idea of a birth trauma. Freud himself had earlier been interested in the subject, suggesting that the anxiety experienced at birth was the prototype for later anxieties. But Rank and Sandor Ferenczi, the Hungarian disciple of Freud, began to carry the work further, reviewing Freudian principles through the lens of the birth trauma. They emphasized the importance of patients acting out and reliving their difficulties at a time when

Freud emphasized the careful study of those difficulties within the transference situation and intellectual insight as the primary therapeutic agents. Differences between Freud and Rank grew—important among them Rank's advocacy of a briefer therapy—culminating in a bitter separation following the publication of *The Trauma of Birth*. Freud saw Rank's theoretical commitment to the birth trauma as a way of avoiding the reality of the Oedipus complex. Freud was also afraid that American pragmatism and success-orientation would turn psychoanalysis into "a watered-down eclectic kind of treatment procedure," and he saw Rank's shortened therapy as "designed to accelerate the tempo of analytic therapy to suit the rush of American life."

In *The Trauma of Birth*, Rank laid out his revision of Freudian theory, explaining how later anxiety like castration anxiety was merely a screen for the primal anxiety of being separated from the mother at birth. All of a patient's reproductions and memories lead back, he argued, to the primal trauma, birth. Rank relates stories of patients of his who, in stuporous, dreamlike states, produced a wealth of material indicating the wish to return to the womb, an obsession with birth, and regressions to a fetal position. Although Rank does not report incidents of primal screaming, his work clearly presages that of Janov in its insistence on a single origin for neurotic anxiety. When Rank writes of something he calls "the healing factor" and of successful therapy as being a question of "severing the Gordian knot of the primal repression with one powerful cut," one begins to picture the theoretical womb out of which Janov's therapy emerged.

Primal Therapy was born decades after the demise of Rank's theory of birth trauma. According to the psychoanalyst Edward Glover, Rank's theory was "officially exploded" in the 1920s, despite rumors that analysts, following the publication of *The Trauma of Birth*, were indeed finding numerous birth traumas in their patients. Modern psychoanalytic thought weighs the birth trauma as simply one of the many possible elements contributing to neurotic behavior, and not as its necessary and ultimate cause. Rank himself, sensing his oversimplification, recognized by 1930 that he had extended his theory "ad absurdum." Freud wrote cunningly of it in 1937: "We have heard little of the clinical results of Rank's plan. Probably it has not accomplished more than would be done if the men of a fire brigade, summoned to deal with a house set on fire by an upset oil-lamp, merely removed the lamp from the room in which the conflagration had broken out. Much less time would certainly be spent in so doing than in extinguishing the whole fire. The theory and practice of Rank's experiment are now things of the past—no less than American 'prosperity' itself."

Freud may have been prophetic about American prosperity, but he sent the birth trauma theory to a premature grave.

Janov's theory, of course, is not built entirely on the premise that there is no cure without reliving one's birth. Only a minority of his patients actually claim to have had their birth Primal. His theory also contains some basic elements of Freudianism, notably the belief in the paramount influence of infantile trauma. Negative feelings that cannot be tolerated by the child are warded off by a wide variety of defenses and symbolic behavior. Neurosis, according to Janov, is nothing more than "the symbolization of Primal Pain . . . the constellation of defenses to cover Primal feelings."

But at this point Janov parts company with Freudian theory. Whereas the latter attempts to understand the neurosis at a matrix of many factors—the child's unconscious wishes, social relations, cultural realities, and the frustration of thwarted impulses—Janov reduces the constellation of factors to only the last, the child's unmet needs. Primal Pain is "the result of parental denial of basic need and natural development." For Janov, Ortiz's cry of "Mommy! Daddy!" says it all. "This," he writes, "leaves no room in our theoretical schema for a mystical force such as the id or an *élan vital*." But it does leave room evidently for a mystical concept called post-Primal Man.

Janov's theory is grounded in a mechanical notion, somewhat similar to that of co-counseling, of behavior that has been called the "hydraulic model" of the psyche. Janov's version is that there is a certain amount of Primal Pain inside us and that if we can just open the pressure valve and let off all the steam, we will be able to overcome all psychological problems. Although Janov denies in print that his theory is reducible to so simple a model—he continually emphasizes the need to make "connections" between past and present feelings—it underlies many of his assumptions. He doesn't believe that the neurotic character is determined by internal conflicts in addition to the struggle between the psyche and the repressive culture that it inhabits; instead he believes that the individual is innately "healthy" and that if the damage wrought by traumatic birth and the withholding of parental love can be undone, one will recover one's inherent wholeness and live somehow outside the restrictions of both society and his own needs. If this is the case, as Janov thinks it is, then defenses become totally unnecessary and anachronistic once this state is achieved.

Freud's grim assumption was that the tension between the individual and his culture could never be completely eradicated, but that through the self-knowledge obtained either in psychoanalysis or by living itself, a person could learn to strike a better balance between the two forces. He would cease expending energy in defending himself against prohibitively painful feelings, once those feelings had been brought to light and examined, and he would then develop a more compassionate understanding of the limitations of the individual. With that understanding, and freed from debilitating symptoms, he would have a better chance of standing up to the dehumanizing potential of society.

For this modest but profound prospect Janov substitutes his monument to total liberation—post-Primal man, a figure so unencumbered that even his unconscious is, in Janov's words, "*real* and healthy."

This sort of speculation reminds one of Norman Vincent Peale and a host of other mind cure personages of the past century who sought to disarm the unconscious by perceiving it as really one's friend, filled constantly with good thoughts. Primal Therapy, so keenly aware on the one hand of the painful nature of the psychological voyage, decides, on the other, to make the trip irresistibly worthwhile by promising that passengers will disembark at a port bathed in virtue, honesty, and health.

The Primal cure, then, is for the patient at last to confront his repressed Pain and exhaust its power over him. But in the way that this is achieved in Primal Therapy, Janov also departs radically from psychoanalytic technique. In psychoanalysis, the therapeutic process is carried out on both a cognitive-intellectual and an emotional plane. The patient, with the help of the analyst's carefully timed offering of insight and interpretation, is led to understand the origins of his feelings and actions. The patient is free to act out in the therapy but is always encouraged to use the adult ego at his disposal to conceptualize his acting out, to perceive it as a disruptive infantile mode of behavior no longer useful to him. By confining the transference—the projection of infantile relationships onto that between patient and therapist—within a clinical context in which it can be analyzed in excruciating detail, the patient may begin to see in what ways he responds to fresh stimuli with petrified attitudes. Of course—and this is the criticism most often lodged against unsuccessful psychoanalysis—if insight is gained only on an intellectual level, psychotherapy will amount to little more than a graduate education in the self without producing any lasting psychological and emotional improvements. But if through arduous, lonely, and painful digging, the patient comes to re-experience and isolate buried perspectives toward his family figures and environment, emancipation from the past becomes increasingly likely. Insight with affect, however, does not accomplish its work in one brutal moment—"Oh my God! You mean—you mean that *I* keep running away from men be-because—oh my God!—Mommy and Daddy abandoned *me* when they got divorced in 1948!" It is not just a single mortar attack launched by the unconscious on the conscious ego, but a siege, full of flak, sniping, strafing, advance and retreat, that the ego must overcome through the most delicate of negotiations.

On the other hand, and it is on this other hand that Janov is inclined to perch himself, if insight is gained primarily through spectacular outbursts of feeling, one runs the risk of getting lost in a compelling *son et lumière* of the past that does not adequately illuminate the surrounding psychic countryside.

In his writings and in the therapy itself, Janov tries to factor out intellectual insight from his therapeutic equation. In psychoanalytic technique, when a patient resists the exposure of a painful feeling, it is not assumed that the patient is consciously concealing anything. His resistance must be analyzed in the context of the transference relationship and in that way force the unconscious feeling into verbal consciousness. But Janov sees this analysis of the resistance as just another defense against "feeling." In fact, he says that the analysis of resistance is just resistance itself. Intellectualizing, which *can* be an insurmountable defense, is disarmed gradually in more traditional psychotherapy where it is remembered that prying prematurely and aggressively is, in therapy as well as life, a sure way not to gain access to the full power of the secret.

In Primal Therapy, however, analysis is thwarted. The therapist, too impatient to negotiate at the border of the patient's consciousness, crashes through the barricade. One former Primal Therapy patient told me that after having a Primal scream in a session with his therapist, he relaxed and began to talk about what he thought had just been happening. "Maybe what I'm doing—" he started, but was cut off by his therapist, who said, "I don't want to head trip with you! I don't want to play that game." Later, during a group session, the patient began to interpret again. Once more, his therapist stopped him, saying, "The only real thing for you to do here is to *be* that little boy. If you start talking to me as an adult, you're wasting your time."

Psychoanalyst Joel Kovel has pointed out the dangers of a therapeutic situation in which the existence of transference is denied. "The fact is," he writes, "that the patient has to be quite aware that he is talking to Janov while fantasizing about his parents. The two streams of thought run together, and the object in each—parents and Janov—comes to represent the other. That the therapist would set going so dramatic an occurrence, then decree that what is in fact happening is really not happening, can only have the effect of recapitulating the image of the omnipotent, reality-defining parent. Further, it skews the communication between the two of them in a way that has powerful emotional consequences." Not only does such a situation amount, according to Kovel, to a variation of Psychologist Gregory Bateson's "double-bind," a confusing, contradictory set of signals, a term originally used by Bateson to explain how families foster psychotic behavior in their children, but it also pretends that only the therapist has access to reality. The patient is almost forcibly infantilized, deprived of all trust in his present perceptions, and a subtle tyranny, dressed as emotional liberation, begins to materialize.

So, for Janov and his patients, then, the expression of a feeling—whether as a Primal scream or a more muted release—would become to a very large extent the basic therapeutic act. If the scream is accompanied by specific memories, images, or ideas, so much the better, but these can have meaning only within the context of the cathartic moment. Years ago, the late psychoanalyst Edward Bibring eloquently expressed the peril of this approach, in which "The production of material and the process of cure are assumed to be identical or coincidental, taking place in one act. Such theoretical reinterpretation," he wrote, "seems apt to circumvent the problem instead of solving it."

One imagines Janov rearing his head at this. Circumvent the problem? You've got to be joking! Janov is convinced he's hitting the heart of it. He's convinced that his method goes so deep it makes Freud look like a mere snorkeler. What does Freud think this is anyway—a coral reef? This is 20,000 Feelings Under the Sea and Janov's been *down* there in his Primal submarine! "We don't recall with emotion—the Freudian abreaction—" Janov says. "We relive. Recall and 'remember' are mind phenomena; relive is a total neurophysiologic one . . . and that is the difference between abreaction and Primals."

4. THE PRIMAL INSTITUTE AS A CHICKEN FARM

Primal Therapy purports to be entirely patient—one might say child—centered. Given Janov's simple interpretation of the origin of neurosis—that the child did not get what he needed from his parents in the past—it comes as no surprise that the patient is expected to express, or Primal, his real needs and Pains and in that fashion get better without the intervention of the therapist. Primal Theory, Janov states, "has validity because it *does not* attempt to imply what drives a specific neurosis. Only a person who experiences a Primal can say what does. Primal Theory simply says that the only validity is *in* experience." Elsewhere, Janov writes that one of the subtle ways "that someone can interrupt the orderly process by which the body sloughs off its Pain . . . is the interpretation that a therapist offers to the patient for his feeling."

One might justifiably receive the impression that Primal Therapists are exceedingly congenial and nondirective—almost, perhaps, high-priced baby-sitters. But if they are that, how does Janov rationalize the costliness of the therapy? And if they are not that, if it *is* their business to facilitate and accelerate growth with well-timed interpretations, clarifications, and attempts to correct what they perceive as the patient's distortions, then in what does their expertise consist?

They are not baby-sitters. Behind the implications of laissez-faire therapy one discovers a most extraordinary arrogance. Janov points out, for instance, that non-primal therapists who come as patients to Primal Therapy discover "that old ideas and techniques were adopted by a neurotic (they were previously neurotic) and were part of their defensive structure." Therapists "want to believe that somehow they have something special to add to the theory and technique. This is not to deny that they often do bring something special to us and the training, but in their neurosis they cannot believe that there is really only one way." Marvin Elder, once the head of therapists' training at the Institute, adds that the trainees agreed that "until they had gotten deep into their own Primal Therapy, *they never really knew what a feeling was.*"

Primal Therapists, Janov claims, "are probably the most highly paid therapists in the country, and for good reason. They have trained long and hard. . . . They are the most skilled therapists in the world." Yet Janov's own daughter was administering therapy while still in her teens and, in at least one case, a severely disturbed female was put in the care of a woman in her early twenties who had only recently been a patient herself! Other therapists in 1972 included a Hollywood actor, a grocery store owner, a New York stage actress—all with no psychological training prior to becoming Primal patients.

Marvin and Ilene Elder had been a psychotherapist team near L.A. until 1970, when, impressed with the first few pages of *The Primal Scream*, they sold their house, gave up their marriage counseling practice, took an income cut from $30,000 to $3,000 the first year, and enrolled at the Institute. The Elders are now alienated from Janov's Primal Institute, where they had undergone the therapy and trained and practiced as therapists. They moved to Kansas City to start their own Primal Center in 1974. Fifteen minutes from downtown Kansas City, it is housed in a one-story building whose rooms the Elders have converted into small sound-proof Primal chambers.

"When I first came to the Institute," Marvin remembers, "it was intellectual paradise, the core of truth of all human existence. It took me a while when I came in to learn that they were just learning themselves. I saw that there was a hope mixed in with Janov's theory—that the theory would include more than it actually did. I really think that Janov believed when he wrote *The Primal Scream* that this *was* the cure for every sort of mental illness. He believed that if you just moved the bottom stone, the whole structure lines itself up in place."

Marvin, who was promoted from patient to therapist in about five months, compares the Institute as it was when he was in residence to "one of those chicken farms in the middle of Chicago" in which special lighting schedules and the use of amphetamines in the feed create an artificial environment that induces chickens to lay more eggs. In this conceit, the eggs are Primal Screams. "By allowing one individual to decide the emphases, not to let different ones come up, no natural balance was achieved. For example," Marvin says, "one of the standard things that used to be done was to have someone stand up in group session and take off his clothes by direction—in effect, to say 'Here I am, naked to the world!' This was supposed to be a sign of achievement!"

"One of the things that got me," Ilene Elder adds, "was that everyone had to admit publicly in group that forever thereafter they are homosexuals. Now that may be part of us—the whole underlying idea of innate bisexuality may be true—but it belittles the Pain to make it into vaudeville."

As for Janov, Marvin says, "He has a great need to be right, to be better than. He also has some deep, pervading Pain, which he avoids. If he, for one second, dropped into that Pain, he said publicly, he would not write for three years."

What is this? The founder of Primal Therapy has cold feet? The Amerigo Vespucci of Primal Pain, the Count of Complete Consciousness, and he's hoarding old hurts, he hasn't leveled with his old Feelings?

The Elders commend Janov's "genius" in "courageously giving up his successful, straight clinical practice" to pursue his Primal discovery. "But," Marvin now says, "he was trying

159

to design it purely intellectually." (The irony is stunning: an anti-intellectual, anti-rational therapy based on an overintellectualized theory.) "At first Janov said there are three basic Primals to have: the birth Primal, the death Primal and—well—the Primal in between. But how can you come up with a scheme like that unless you're fishing with your head? So I would say that although Art's got a good fast head and can see relationships and connections, he didn't have the benefit of being connected himself while he was creating what he was creating. The tragedy is that if this same guy had been in Pain and feeling and suffering and had his head as well, he wouldn't have made such gross mistakes." As for the other therapists at the Institute, Marvin feels that "some of them were automatons, judging from the way they'd follow Janov's instructions."

Ron, our Primal patient from Boston, had numerous experiences that suggest Janov was less than spontaneous in his reactions, that he had not truly achieved the Absence of Significant Blocking Pain. Ron was once hugging a female patient in the Institute when Janov walked by and announced: "Carver, you're acting out." Ron, already by this time accustomed to Janov's behavior, simply ignored the comment. Janov warned: "I'm deadly serious."

"Well," Ron replied. "You can *be* deadly serious," throwing back at Janov the kind of Primal remark therapists often use to encourage "feelings" in patients. Janov became angry. The woman Ronnie had been hugging took off. Janov kept on. "Look," Ron finally said. "I've had a Primal today and I'm here because I just want to be with other people."

"Just because you've had your Primal for today," Janov retorted, "doesn't mean you can keep on acting out tonight."

Ron felt the whole thing was getting out of hand and fell silent, but Janov wanted the last word.

"Whenever we get into an argument," he said, "I'm always right and you're always wrong."

Another patient once found himself in the Institute elevator with Janov. "You seem tense," the patient said to him. "No!" Janov replied. "*You're* the one who's unreal."

5. PRIMAL PSYCHOBABBLE

In his first book, Janov stressed that Primal Therapy did not use terminology to label people nor did it diagnose. This may be true to the extent that Primal Therapy has abandoned psychiatric vocabulary and diagnostic categories in talking *about* patients. But what Primal Therapy does is employ a standardized set of responses and interpretations *with* the patient; these phrases constitute a method of referring to the universal childhood feelings that Primal Therapy holds to be the source of all neurotic adult behavior.

In principle, this particular form of psychobabble is designed constantly to reveal the latent meaning of a patient's words and actions *to* the patient. It often has the effect of causing the person to whom it is addressed to break down in tears or a Primal, to elicit "feeling." Primal Therapy's psychobabble is not defined by idle statements of purpose, as when someone remarks, "I've just got to get my head together"; instead it does get at certain emotions by revealing verbal conduct as merely a mask for ulterior wishes and needs. In this way, Primal Therapy's phraseology tries to uncover, in Eric Berne's terms, the "operation" behind the "game." One "game" the patient might play is to tell the therapist: "You're stupid and can't understand a word I'm saying to you!" The therapist might point out that the operation behind the accusation, the need for reassurance, might more truthfully be expressed on its own terms by saying: "I feel insecure and want to be reassured by you." (Of course there are other possibilities: the patient may be very poor at self-expression or else the therapist may, compared to the patient, *be* stupid. This last eventuality would throw the whole game out of whack by pointing out a more pressing and present problem in their communication.)

In Primal Therapy, the operation behind the game is assumed to be a childhood need or transaction. For instance, one Primal patient asked his therapist, in reference to an invitation he received: "Do you think it's okay for me to come to this party?" The therapist, sniffing the latent meaning, retorted: "I'm not your Daddy!"

In principle, then, this kind of response has it uses. It constantly tries to align a patient's manifest behavior with its original meaning. But in Primal Therapy it is used so frequently and as a matter of course that it becomes a game itself, and one that cannot always sort out the deep infantile meaning of a statement from what may be a more immediate and legitimate purpose. For example, the person above might actually not know from the information available to him whether he was really welcome at the party and so, although the person may at the same time seem to be evincing his generally neurotic dependency, the response "I'm not your Daddy!" tends to rob him too completely of the present reality. It plunges him head first into his unconscious, a place that, unlike a cold swimming pool, is usually best entered gradually, and from the shallow end. In fact, the exchange between the party-going patient and the therapist took place not in the latter's office but on the corner of Melrose and Almont in Los Angeles.

But the psychobabble of Primal Therapy is hyperbolic and its nature is often to collar patients into having insights about themselves. To this end, Primal Therapy utilizes, among others, the following stock phrases:

The "Fuck Off": This expletive is employed to indicate to a patient that his intellectualization, defense, rationalization, or explanation is not needed, that it interferes with a therapy interested only in "feelings." During one group session, Ron watched while a therapist had his own Primal concerning how he hated Ron. If Ron had ventured to interrupt the therapist's Primal with his "defense," that would have been "ripping-off" the therapist's "feelings," so he waited until the dramatics were over before asking, "Will you let me tell you what I think is happening?"

"Fuck off!" the therapist told him, indicating that any commentary would still be a rip-off of his feelings.

The "Never Enough": This is a stock phrase expressing the sad truth that one can never really get what one needed in the past as a child trying to deal with a "nongiving world." For instance, a patient complained about a friend: "He got mad at me for forgetting his birthday!" The therapist consoled him: "Never enough, is it?" referring to how hard it is to please others and fulfill their infantile needs. Ron once remarked that this particular line is used so predictably that it carries all the weight of "Have a good day."

The "Who Is It Really?": The basic trigger for a patient's Deep Feeling. "I'm really pissed at you for what you did Saturday night!" the patient yells at the therapist. "Who is it really?" the therapist responds. "MOMMY!" the patient cries wildly and, the connection made, drops into a Primal.

The "Be Afraid": An example of the Go With the Feeling school of thought—or feeling. One woman called her friend, who was in Primal Therapy: "I think there's a prowler outside," she said, frightened. "I'm really afraid. What should I do?" "Stay with yourself," she is told. "Be afraid." Ideally, going with one feeling should lead to other, deeper, Primal ones.

The "That's a Feeling": An all-purpose interpretation designed to distinguish between what's a feeling and whatever it is that isn't; a method of getting the patient to "Cop to a Feeling." For example: "You are the most insensitive asshole I've ever met," the patient says.

"That's a feeling," the therapist points out.

The "Who Else Said (Looked at You Like, Treated You Like, etc.) That?": Like the "Who Is It Really?" this fosters connections between conscious and unconscious material and, in one form or another, is used in probably all psychodynamic therapies. "Joe," says the patient, "when I saw you Sunday night in the car, you just stared at me. What's wrong?" "Who else looked at you like that?" says Joe, his therapist. At this point, the patient might elect to point out that he had anticipated precisely that response and is bored by saying, 'My father used to look at me like that when I slurped my soup' and then having a Primal. But the therapist will be ready for him. He says: "Look, I'm not going to head-trip with you."

One of the reasons that Marvin and Ilene Elder say they broke with Janov and the Institute had to do with Janov's reliance on a rigid psychobabble and the way it interfered with early feelings that couldn't, in their minds, be verbalized at all. The Elders and their faction came to be known as the First-Liners, in reference to their heavier emphasis on early, birth-oriented Pain; Janov's loyalists were called the Feelers. Marvin Elder, who, according to Ron, his former patient, was at one time an accomplished psychobabbler, has now changed his views and thinks that if he were to say to a patient who was having a Deep Feeling, "Tell Mommy," he would be "an asshole of the first order. One of the first flaws that came through to me at the Institute," he now says, "was how I began thinking in a glossary of terms. Once, one was used on me. Another therapist used the word 'dyke' which, believe it or not, I didn't know at the time. So I came to be known as a 'dork,' someone who doesn't know anything."

"What really got to me," Ilene says, "was the use of labels. You know, here you have this 'post-Primal patient' and until you behave the way he behaves you're a 'suck.' Now what's that got to do with me?"

Some nonverbal gestures are also used in consistent, predictable ways, particularly the Shrug. The Shrug is the nonverbal equivalent of the "You Can't Get That Here," which means that patients at the Institute can't get there what they never got as children, but can only and finally *feel* that they didn't get it then and can't get it now. In other words, while being provided with pillows, cribs, and a support system for their regressions, they are simultaneously reminded that they are *not* children, that the Institute is not just some *big tit* they can *suck*. So when a Primal patient is needing something, the therapist might just Shrug. Ron remembers one therapist, now head of the San Francisco branch of the Institute, as being the Shrugger par excellence. He would look to the sky, hold out his arms, palms up, raise his shoulders, and there was no question at all but that You Can't Get That Here.

6. THE POLITICS OF PRIMALING

"The beginning of feeling is the end of philosophy," Janov writes, making a distinction between emotions and reason. Sam Wolfe, another Primal Therapist, adds that "Long-standing Primal patients exhibit little or no interest in philosophies." Wolfe goes on to say that most people believe the truths about their lives "must be shrouded in mystery.

It's almost as neurotic as the idea that the more complex the explanation, the greater the truth contained therein."

Is it all so simple in the end? Is it true that the more you feel—or scream—the less you have to think? Janov, to be sure, is aware in his writing that the ballgame is more complicated: "There are those who imagine that it is '*Primal Scream* Therapy' and that all patients have to do is scream or let out their anger or tears," he warned in 1974. "Crying is not necessarily feeling; it can often just mean release or catharsis. *Connection* is the thing." This sounds quite reasonable. So maybe one doesn't have to scream oneself to post-Primaldom. After all this, is the scream part of it only incidental? What does Janov mean? That the scream is necessary but not sufficient? When he addresses the question, he seems to want to ride his horse in both directions: "The scream is what some people do when in Pain; others react differently to Pain. In any case, it works from inside out, not the outside in; so a patient must scream as a result of felt Pain, not scream as an exercise to get to feeling. He must not scream or do anything like that as a result of some dictum of a therapist. Indeed, the hallmark of mock Primal Therapy is the authoritarian structure in which therapists in some way manipulate, order, and control the patient."

In light of these comments, it would be well to listen to some of Ron's reflections on his own Primal experiences: "The assumption at the Primal Institute, and an incredible one now that I'm away from it, was that here are a bunch of people supposedly fucked-up who, after one or two weeks of Primal Therapy—three hours a day—are supposed to go into a group session, into a room with maybe fifty people lying around and screaming, and then reveal their most intimate feelings in front of them. And me, I had a lot of Pain—just to use the jargon—about showing my feelings at all. That's what I was there to work on, and after a week or two I'm already supposed to be able to do that, to the point where, if it makes me feel bad not to be able to, I'm supposed to Primal about *that*. Now remember, at this stage, I don't even know what a Primal is and I was later to recognize that the situation was too much for me; I was so unready for it that of course I couldn't let go of my feelings. I tensed up against it and did the opposite. It made me feel like I was in summer camp, and other kids could tie a slip knot and I couldn't. And I couldn't Primal about it. So Primal Therapy was becoming goal-oriented, Primaling a performance activity, so I began to focus on 'I can't do it' as an activity rather than as an expression of my feelings.

"The trouble is that lip service is paid to the opposite. When I got there I was told to go at my own pace, don't rush, in fact you're made to feel fucked-up if you *have* to have a Primal right away. Yet, there is a subtle pressure there, and people who do have Primals right away are extolled as being natural and good. I remember once when a patient got up in group and began to shout about another woman, 'She's only been here two weeks and she's having a Primal already! I've been here eight months and I can't have a Primal!' And that's honestly how he felt but it wasn't going to get him anywhere, it wasn't the kind of hurting conducive to change. It was absurd.

"People would fight over the pillows that you were assigned to take to group with you—they were also your personal pillows to take home with you, the idea being that none of these people *had* anything when they were little so now we're going to give them something. Now, one time, a friend who didn't know about the pillows because it was her first group, walked in, saw a pillow, took it, lay down and had a serious Primal during the middle of which some guy comes over and looms over her and screams, 'You took my pillow!' You took my pillow!' See, he was looking for any excuse to get out some feeling, so it looks good—oh! he's really free, he's able to Primal, but to me now it seems ludicrous. He shouldn't have been there to cry about his pillow. Situations would spiral in a certain way—enough things were provided to get mad at so you can always feel like you're getting something out, but I know that I didn't ever feel like I was getting what I needed there.

"Because of the nature and location of the Institute, a lot of actors and actresses came, among them one who, at a suspiciously propitious moment in group, went into a remarkable birth Primal, or so it appeared. It could be that she was merely incorporating her need to perform, her acting ability, into the format of what appeared to be a Primal. Her Primals were quite remarkable; she always started by talking about the daughter she had with another actor, then she would fall to her knees sobbing, then go into a birth primal. Frankly, I didn't believe her. There's no way of proving it, of course. Probably, if it wasn't real, it was *unconsciously* not real.

"I was aware from the beginning that things weren't quite right. Other people who were better than I at imitating weren't so aware of it. One guy named Rodney went on for months Primaling, having all these memories. He was getting there so fast! But after a while I realized he was the same obnoxious asshole as before, actually worse because he was now more confident. His therapist finally said to him in group, 'I don't think what you're doing is real,' which was probably true but didn't leave him anywhere. Then, two weeks later, he comes in and announces, 'Oh, that was all bullshit, my Primals.' But what really turned me around was that he had had exact memories about what had happened to him when he was three, and to me that's a very subtle kind of performance.

168

"Another woman appeared to have good Primals, writhing on the floor, having memories with images. I don't know what that means, but Janov assumes that if you do that, you're resolving things. Now if you do something that looks like that, you *might* be resolving things, but she had taken a lot of acid trips and maybe certain neurological connections were opened up because of the acid, maybe she wasn't having connections that resolved anything, but was just reliving something by acting out.

"Now, I had that Primal back in New York before Primal Therapy, and it seemed natural to me. So when I left my job, and came to the West Coast where I was told not to see anybody and had very few physical outlets, I thought 'Oh my God, all this deep pain is going to come out. Am I man enough to feel it?' I had a lot of difficulty at first, but didn't think to attribute it to the fact that the circumstances were so strange that I couldn't feel anything. Instead I began to believe, 'Oh my God, I have so much Primal Pain I can't even begin to deal with it!' And that is what happens to every single person there, in different ways.

"I was talking about my parents one day during individual therapy with Marvin and he said, 'Sink into your feelings,' and immediately I pictured myself on a rowboat sinking into the water. I didn't know what he was talking about. But I knew I was supposed to come up with something right then. Now *that* I could feel, that much I still had left. So I tried to make appropriate noises and I found that I could do that, to my horror, and that most people could make all sorts of crying, gasping noises. Where before it was natural that one time in New York, now it was a situation in which I *wanted* to have Primals. How can you *want* to have a Primal?

"There were many like me and we all got together like one miserable clique; we were the ones who couldn't and sat

around and talked about the ones who could. And we didn't
even know if the others could or couldn't, just that they were
able to make different kinds of noises."

7. LAUREN

Janov's therapy, advanced as "The Cure for Neurosis,"
looked like the perfect therapeutic recourse for those whom
other psychotherapies, consciousness-raising organizations,
and the pharmaceutical industry had failed. Still, Janov
writes that he tries to screen out "the brain-damaged and
severe psychotics." Maybe functioning neurotics were only a
scream away from happiness (to use the title of a book by
New York group scream therapy innovator Dr. Daniel
Casriel), but who was to say those whose lives were more
nightmarish would also be helped? Feeling their Pain was
perhaps something they had already mastered all too well.

In practice, though, there was a problem; the Institute's
rather idiosyncratic diagnostic technique—which had more to
do with taking the depth measure of the individual's Primal
pool of Pain and dropping him into it than with determining
beforehand how well the patient might be able to swim un-
derwater—lent it, once in a while, to taking on more than it
could handle.

One former therapist, who had risen to that status after
only five months as a patient and despite the fact that by his
own admission he had not yet had a Primal, recalls that
Janov once berated him for going too easy on a patient—for
not, in the lingo, "busting" him. The next day, he says, he
was much harder on the patient, who did not then have a
feeling for a week.

In regard to Primal Therapy's fanatic hankering after the
psychological truth, an anecdote of Otto Rank's is useful

170

here. Rank was once paid a visit by an unmarried thirty-five-year-old woman who had suffered excruciating intestinal attacks every couple of weeks for eight years. After numerous consultations with physicians, she had concluded she was the victim of an emotional problem. She told Rank that she was well-adjusted. She had never, though, fallen in love or married and now lived with her married sister. Rank listened. Finally he told her to keep her stomach trouble. Privately, he did not know what serious difficulties lay beneath her cramps and figured that her symptom was perhaps a small price to pay for the ordeal of living. Her defense mechanisms, after all, were working. If one penetrated them too zealously, an awful wealth of psychic disturbance might have been revealed, and to no one's particular benefit. The woman would then experience a sense of deprivation far greater than that caused by her physical symptoms, and one for which she would sense, at her age and in her position, there was no relief at all. "In other words," Rank said, "it is not so much a question as to whether we are able to cure a patient, whether we can or not, but whether we should or not."

Now, perhaps Rank was playing it overly safe or else submitting to cultural pressures in thinking that an unmarried thirty-five-year-old woman could not find greater contentment, even through psychoanalysis, but we cannot know this for sure. What is apparent, however, is a more universal point. People are entitled to the pursuit of happiness, but they shouldn't necessarily be led on a pursuit that, given the limitations of both the human being and the social milieu, has little chance of succeeding. Not everyone needs to be analyzed. Not everyone can be. The "cure," in one sense, consists precisely in the individual's reconciliation to that modest extent to which he or she can grow. To pretend that there are no boundaries to that space invites disaster.

This is perhaps a distressing thought for America's cult of

candor and personal renaissance; one does not want to have to sit down at the bargaining table with one's own ideals and hammer out a reasonable contract for change. In Primal Therapy the atmosphere of conciliation was negligible indeed.

Lauren was in some ways the victim of Primal Therapy, to which she turned as a last resort. But neither Primal Therapy nor the Institute can really be said to have caused what happened. Many of those close to Lauren, including Ron, the closest person of all in her last few years, seem to feel that the final chapter had been written long ago.

Lauren suffered from nothing as tolerable and regular as fortnightly intestinal trouble. She did not suffer from a severe physical symptom that hinted at deeper irresolutions, unfinished Oedipal business which, if left uncompleted, would still have enabled her to function well. Instead, Lauren had few defenses left at all; like a pocket turned inside out, she had nothing to hide because there was no place to hide it. When Lauren arrived for Primal Therapy in 1972 at the age of twenty-six, it was the last stop on a long tour of psychiatrists and therapists.

"It turned out in Lauren's case," Marvin Elder said, looking back, "that at the Institute there was no separate way of thinking to deal with her, no allowance made for excesses."

One of the criteria for admitting patients at the time was their ability to cry. Lauren thought this was a terrible mistake from the beginning, long before she had any other complaints about the Institute. She knew that crying itself was not necessarily a sign of proximity to one's feelings. She knew; she had been doing it constantly for years and she didn't feel any better.

Lauren's father had left home in his teens to begin a long Army career. He rose quickly in rank despite having only an eighth grade education. Three days before the end of World War II he was hit in the head by a bomb fragment and spent three years recovering in a hospital. In 1946 Lauren was born, the second of five children. The father ran the home like a military camp, devising signals to summon each child. Lauren's signal was two rings of a bell in his study. She was expected to obey all his wishes—from shining his shoes to serving him tea—and disobedience meant a hit on the head. The father himself suffered continually from severe headaches; it was thought to be a miracle that he had survived the wound at all. But authoritarianism was not a trait of the father alone; Bob, the firstborn, once talked back to his mother and she kept him in the house for an entire summer. Donna, a younger sister, says her mother was "diabolical, loving one day, remote the next, full of paradoxical communications." The father at least was consistent; though violent, he always acted as if he loved his children.

Lauren consciously remembered one particular aspect of her childhood. Between the ages of eleven and a half and fifteen, her father molested her sexually virtually every day by playing with her breasts and making her lie on a bed with him while he scrutinized photographs of naked women. He threatened to beat her if she did not obey. At fifteen she began crying hysterically, often to the point where she couldn't breathe. The father finally became disgusted and the seductions ended. He now denies that this ever happened and once insisted to her that, "I never laid a hand on your head." Still, much later, when Lauren was in her twenties, he told her over the phone that he was "not responsible for what I did to you after the war." And Bob, the older brother, remembered his saying to Lauren, "I was just doing that to prepare you for the world."

The father had become a magician when Lauren was four, often working as many as five shows a day in Italy, where the family was stationed. He specialized in illusions, to say the least. He enjoyed pulling reality out from under his audience's feet. Lauren and Bob, the two oldest, grew up to have certain problems apprehending reality. Bob, for instance, who also went through Primal Therapy, once backed up his car in a parking lot, narrowly missing another. The driver of the other car got out and claimed that he had been hit. Bob knew he hadn't made contact, but the driver insisted. Eventually, Bob "felt his reality slipping away" and could no longer determine whether he had or hadn't.

For Lauren, life would later seem like a series of devastatingly disorienting tricks played on her by an illusionist. She would say that her parents made a habit of altering history right in front of their children's eyes. It was not merely a question of disguising feelings, common enough, but rather of sometimes denying physical reality. Childhood was something of a *trompe l'oeil*. No less was it hard work. Family life was totally regimented and responsibilities were passed onto the eldest children prematurely. From the age of six on, Lauren found herself taking regular care of her younger siblings. At nine she had a paper route and at thirteen was required to pay for her own contact lenses to retard what an optometrist said was a process that would lead eventually to blindness. Although she was supporting herself later at the University of Minnesota, her father claimed her as a dependent, thus preventing her from getting a scholarship, which she badly needed. At twenty-one, she took custody of her younger siblings after her mother had become frightened for their welfare during the father's periods of anger.

As an adolescent, Lauren believed that she had "God inside her" and talked with Him every day about how rotten things were. She sensed she had been set on earth to be a martyr. She was going to be a saint. It was the only way to reconcile her life with living.

At nineteen, she met a graduate student at Minnesota; she felt she had found a platonic, kindred spirit. In fact, she thought he too was a saint. At this point, Lauren was functioning, but slept very little, often working as a piano player in a bar. She was also nothing less than a brilliant student. Her undergraduate papers on Shakespeare demonstrate a precocious critical intellect that was duly acknowledged by her professors. The papers are extremely articulate, but also rather bloodless.

After a few months of close friendship with her comrade, they once kissed good night, an act which for Lauren, who had had no genital sensation as an adolescent, had no romantic undertow. From then on, however, he made a conscious effort to convince Lauren that she had been trying to seduce him and that therefore they should sleep together. This contradiction of her version of reality was the trigger that produced her first serious breakdown. A year later, when she had already lost the ability to speak spontaneously and had to memorize even the simplest salutation, the graduate student admitted to her that he had been trying to "fuck her over," but by then she was in very bad shape. The breakdown had been gradual, complicated by sleeping pills that prohibited her from dreaming normally for six months. She started having nightmares that would plague her from then on. They were, in her phrase, "physical dreams" indistinguishable from reality. If she dreamed she was in love with someone, she could not shed that feeling in waking life for several days.

She visited various psychotherapists but could only cry in front of them. She had been crying convulsively for a couple of hours a day since childhood. She would go five days without sleep. Any rejection, even at the hands of a total stranger, would cause her to become suicidal. Once she had built herself up a little with the help of a woman friend, she began to live a life of frantic desperation. The quotidian became a matter of life and death. She sought out relationships, hoping to be swallowed up in another person. She lived with three or four men consecutively. She cried constantly. She renounced God for people, sainthood for pick-ups at local bars.

The last man she lived with before entering Primal Therapy was familiar with bio-energetic techniques. He told her one day to bend over backwards, breathe deeply, and say "No." As a child, Lauren had not been allowed to say "No" and now, when she was able to do so after a struggle, she was overtaken by screams. She screamed uncontrollably for five minutes and then couldn't remember at all what had happened. Then, during her last year at Minnesota, she began to do a form of Primal Therapy regularly. Before long, she found that words came involuntarily out of her mouth: "Goddy, Goddy. Daddy, Daddy."

She flew out to Los Angeles for an interview with the head therapist at the Institute. She was accepted and went back to Minnesota where she raised the $6,000 fee.

In June, 1972, Lauren, at the age of twenty-six, arrived at the Institute on a Tuesday. Her therapy was to begin the following Monday but she became so desperate that she had to start immediately and was given as a therapist not someone with clinical experience with psychotics, but Nancy, a woman in her early twenties with no clinical experience at all beyond her brief indoctrination at the Institute. Like many others, Nancy had been drawn to Primal Therapy because she was overintellectualized and in Pain. In 1970 she had seen *The Primal Scream* in the New Arrival section of her city's public library, taken it home, read it, and begun crying.

Like Lauren's father, Nancy's was a career military man who ran his house "like a barracks." The two women had a number of other things in common. Nancy had been molested around puberty and, although clearly not suffering like Lauren, she had been pathologically afraid of men and had once seriously contemplated suicide. Immediately, Nancy took Lauren into one of the sound-proofed rooms and Lauren began Primaling. For a while, Lauren wanted to work only with Nancy. However, she didn't feel that she was "in the same kind of Pain" as she had been and would tell Nancy, "I'm not Primaling the way I used to at Minnesota." Nancy would say, according to Lauren, that a Primal could be this or that, not to worry about it, just get the feeling out. "It looks fine," she would say about Lauren's efforts.

About two months into the therapy, Lauren began to experience baby talk again, screaming words like "Goddy" and "Daddy." Nancy intervened to suggest that Lauren's father might have raped her. Lauren insisted that he had only molested her. Nancy said she was only trying to help her feel the feeling.

Strangely, in September of 1972, Lauren began to have Primals that felt to her like rape, and the nature of her baby talk seemed to confirm that she had been. After all, if she was Primaling that she had been raped, wasn't it more than likely she *had* been? And even if Nancy *had* suggested the rape scene with her father, certainly Lauren would not have been susceptible to the rape suggestion if it hadn't happened? While she screamed, she experienced a pain in her vagina and anus; Lauren did not at first connect this physical pain with any memory, but then there was the baby talk— "No, Daddy, no! No kickie baby!"—and also Nancy's suggestions.

That summer of 1972, Ron met Lauren at the Institute. Both of them had been there only a short while. Ron, who had already begun to tire a little of Primal Therapy's subtle totalitarianism—but not enough so to abandon his hopes and the largest part of his six grand—found in Lauren one of the few individuals there who was not caught up entirely in the Primal way of life. But he was at the same time afraid of how disturbed she was, how fragile. He was reluctant to ask her out. Most of the people at the Institute could not see her in that light; they were too concerned with the fact that she could Primal easily and they couldn't. If Primals were the accepted measure of psychological progress, then she was well on her way to post-Primaldom.

Ron could see that her miserable life made his, by comparison, seem like the first twenty minutes of *Bambi*. He had a hard time being around her, but nonetheless sought to help her out; once he bought her a set of drawing markers. Lauren walked around each morning until one, when she had a session at the Institute. Afterward, she would rest and attend a group session in the evening. That was her life; it was, for the long moment, one tedious boxstep.

In October, Ron flew back East for a week. By that time, he had begun to feel at home at the Institute. He would later see that he had really only learned "how to do the therapy," as if it were just a game one mastered, but then he proudly felt that he *knew* about feelings and that those outside of Primal Therapy were lost, confined by Significant Blocking Pain. He spent a couple of days with his parents, who were astonished when their thirty-one-year-old son began berating them for messing up his life. The three of them became quite upset, and Ron's mother began crying.

"*You* can cry," Ron yelled at her, "and *I* can't yet!" He realized suddenly that he was less angry at her than at himself. Five months at the Institute and he hadn't shed one good tear.

On his return, Ron and Lauren made an arrangement. She would work with Ron two hours a day to try and get him to have a Primal; then he would "sit" for her two hours a day. It was obvious by now that she couldn't depend entirely on Nancy.

For the next three months, they "sat" for each other. Most of the time Lauren seemed to be working out the rape scene, re-enacting it physically on the floor of the womblike Primal room. She would have convulsions—"rape contractions," as she called them—while lying on her stomach, her legs kicking and one arm twisted behind her back. It was very convincing. Ron sat a yard away on the carpeted floor, silent, sympathetic.

Lauren then passed from the rape material into something else, Primals concerning her mother and how, in her anxiety and horror over what was happening to Lauren because of the father, she had tried to strangle Lauren. This too she acted out repeatedly.

Lauren continued to need vast amounts of personal attention beyond the three-week intensive therapy. Other patients had settled into their group regimen, but Lauren was still desperate. The therapists' alarm was mitigated, however, by their knowledge that Ron was working more and more with her.

Ron left the Institute in January of 1973 to return to the teaching post which had been reserved for him. When he paid a quick return visit to L.A. in February, he found that Lauren had entered a new stage. "I'm in unreality," she said.

Reluctantly, Ron flew back East and in March received a phone call from Lauren saying that she couldn't Primal any more and had developed severe symptoms: she couldn't urinate, defecate, or sleep. She was taking fifteen chloral hydrate capsules at a time. She needed more help right away. The Institute, instead of giving her more sessions, was giving her more pills. Ron offered to fly out for a week during the coming spring vacation, but she was too desperate and he finally said she could fly to New York. He was still frightened of her emotional fragility, but he sensed that the Institute was not helping her now.

Just before coming East, she entered yet another stage. She was, as she put it, "in paranoia." She could not be around other people without vomiting. Nancy said that it was all part of Primal Therapy, just go with it. The attitude of the Institute was that one opened oneself up as much as possible and then caught up to the feeling. That was okay if you were treading water in the deep end, but Lauren was by this point lying at the bottom of the pool, and the lifeguard was looking in the other direction.

One day, "in paranoia," Lauren saw a shadow on the pavement on her way to the bank and she panicked, literally paralyzed for an instant. She finally flew to New York where she discovered that she now needed four hours of Primaling a day. On the second night in Ron's apartment, she couldn't sleep. Rolling in pain on the floor, baby-talking uncontrollably, she was experiencing something that was no longer part of the Primal, or if it was, then it had to be said that her life was becoming one long Primal. Ron was terrified. He couldn't tell her to go back to L.A.; she could barely move. Besides, they were more and more involved emotionally, not just in the Primal sense, but in a sexual, more conventional way. What am I going to do, Ron thought; he felt unimaginably alone.

Before leaving the Institute, Lauren had gone before a therapist and said, aren't you going to give me any help, and he had not said anything in particular but had made a lot of eye contact with the floor and said, why don't you go see Ron? This was a contradiction of Primal policy; believing that they alone could practice Primal Therapy, the therapists did not ordinarily want patients to go elsewhere to do it. But they had, implicitly at the very least, failed with Lauren. Instead of suggesting a professional who specialized in severe disorders, they just let her go off to Ron.

"Frankly," Marvin Elder had once said to Ron about his caring for Lauren, "we're grateful that you're doing this."

A therapist told him, "You know, you're running a small hospital."

After Lauren's night of rolling on the floor, the two of them tried something new. She was still "in paranoia," and couldn't bear physically or emotionally to be near anyone, including Ron, so he would go into the next room. In this way, she was able to Primal. If they were together in one room, Lauren couldn't breathe, would baby-talk incessantly, even forget who Ron was. Eventually he rented a Primal room for her nearby and would drive her over, but just being in the car with Ron provoked a paranoid reaction.

Meanwhile, medical problems began to mount. A severe duodenal ulcer plagued her. She was constipated for three weeks before finally collapsing. But she refused to go to a doctor because she couldn't be in the presence of another person. Catastrophic as the situation had become, Ron respected her wishes. Among his reasons for rejecting the possibility of outside professional help was his continuing belief in the Primal gospel and the partial successes they experienced using it. There was a strong sense that it was the two of them against a hostile world, that theirs was a Primal bond no third party could violate. An only child who had spent a relatively reclusive adolescence, Ron pursued a new kind of solitude with Lauren.

During the summer, she needed to Primal four and five hours a day, which left Ron precious little time for anything besides his teaching. He would "sit" for her for an hour or more, give her a sleeping pill, and, while she rested, teach his class before returning for another session.

In the fall of 1973, Ron began enlisting the aid of friends to help Lauren. He even put ads in a local paper offering to pay people to "sit" for her. One friend went to Ron's apartment once every few weeks for a while; there he would find Lauren in a small room at the back which Ron had soundproofed against her screams by tacking up scraps of carpet on the walls and ceiling. When the friend entered the room, illuminated only by a single lamp on the floor, he would find Lauren lying on her back in a loose shirt, jeans, and heavy sweat socks. A small woman, she had become even thinner now. The carpet was littered with used Kleenex from the day's previous Primals, tissues into which she had coughed up the sputum liberated by her catharses.

The room, devoid of all furniture but the one chair into which Ron's friend lowered himself, was humid, almost sweet-smelling. Lauren and the man would begin by talking generally for a bit; once they became engaged in a discussion about French movie directors. She had strong, sensitive opinions about both Jean-Luc Godard and François Truffaut. Although she had ceased reading books now that Primaling took up most of her waking life, she was vastly intelligent and tossed in thoughtful references to French phenomenology, which she had studied intensively in graduate school.

There might be a pause in the conversation, a certain nervous anticipation on the man's part, and Lauren would say she felt like Primaling now, was that okay? Ron's friend would nod and she would begin to breathe very deeply, soon calling out about "Mommy" or "Daddy" as she exhaled. She seemed to gather a momentum and her baby talk would increase in both volume and pace. "Mommy, Mommy, lookie baby, talkie baby." She would begin to writhe pain-fully on the floor and, while appearing to re-enact the rape scene, she would assume the position of a figure being raped from behind. Her body seemed to take over; she bounced up and down on the floor, rolled over, all the while alternating between baby talk and rasping, piercing screams.

After ten or fifteen minutes of this, the Primal would ebb. Then she would ask Ron's friend if he was all right and if it upset him at all, what she was doing. She might begin to talk in normal, earnest tones about what she had just been Primaling, whether it was her father's repeated rape of her or her mother sticking pins into her body when she was two years old. Then, shortly, she would announce that she would like to go on and, almost as soon as she had got the words out, would plunge back into her Primaling. It was tiring for the man to watch her; she was like a woman in excruciating labor, trying to give birth over and over again to her mon-strous memories.

Lauren's progress was slow—it would take her months to "complete" a scene through Primaling—and Ron's was often even slower since he was devoting literally all his free time to Lauren. But together, devoted to Primal Therapy even if they had given up on the Primal Institute, they struggled to gain for Lauren some relief from her sense of unreality, and more than just relief, they convinced themselves that by allowing Lauren's Primal Pain to work itself out—she would once again recapture her health. They would recapture it themselves, without assistance from the outside world, for that outside world, they had both come to believe while at the Institute, was completely out of touch with feeling and could never understand the rare beauty of their private thera-peutic plan.

The amazing thing was that Lauren, over time, did get better in many respects. Over a nine-month period in 1973, she went from needing four and five hours of Primaling a day to seven and eight and then, miraculously, down to two and three. She went from twenty sleeping pills a day to eight. There was reason to believe that her store of Primal Pain was dwindling fast. Many of her symptoms had vanished: her ulcer had healed completely, her menstrual periods had become regular for the first time in her life, she grew two inches in height, and her posture improved. By early winter of 1973, she was no longer "in paranoia." She was functioning better, had lost her terror around other people, could make love with more feeling and sensation than ever. She dressed well again. Her physical coordination improved. She now began doing yoga, dancing, playing frisbee with Ron, going to the movies. On a trip back to L.A., she accompanied Ron and a friend to a hockey game at the Los Angeles Forum where she sat among 16,000 fans and felt fine. It was remarkable. The system is working, Ron thought. It was different from Janov's, more total. They didn't use teddy bears and pillows to simulate childhood Gestalts, but they used everything—records, movies, television, anything at all in the present—to get at their old feelings. Theirs was a complete symbiotic therapeutic relationship. They were the real pioneers on the Primal frontier.

Things were looking up early in 1974. But then the floor gave way again. Symptoms redeveloped. When they went out, Lauren would say that her whole world was disintegrating. It was like her father's magic show all over again; now you see it, now you don't. She was lost in a terrifying schizophrenic discontinuity between her physical body and her symbolic self. She quite literally did not know where she stood in the world. Nothing was familiar. All of experience hit a nerve.

Her body produced too many symptoms when Ron was around, so he moved out of his own apartment and remained on twenty-four-hour call for her. By May he didn't feel right about anything. Though a much stronger person than she, he began almost to acquire some of her symptoms. He too began to share her extreme vulnerability, her distrust of the world. He could no longer see what Lauren was doing to other people, to himself, to herself; he could only see what others were doing to her.

Lauren began to teach a yoga class, but Ron had to Primal her beforehand, leave her alone for half an hour, and then go over after her class to Primal her again. In desperation, she flew back to the Institute in L.A. but was denied any special help, "for her own good." Ron followed her out in June. Her need to Primal was back up to eight hours a day, a full-time job for both of them. At first, they interpreted the increase as her body's effort to get out the last of the Primal material as fast as possible, but it continued and continued. For Ron, the word "nightmare" didn't begin to describe his existence. For the next year and a half, he Primaled her eight hours a day. And when he wasn't Primaling her, he was making sure the conditions were right for her next Primal. The outside world had to be kept at arm's length from her at all times or she couldn't Primal at all. If someone called her on the phone and upset her, it was he who would have to call the individual back and correct the situation, regardless of whether there had originally been an insult or not. At this point, there was nothing that was not an insult to her central nervous system. Lauren would catch some sleep when she could and as soon as she woke up, often in the middle of the night, she would call Ron at the room he sublet so that she could be alone, and he would Primal her.

By the summer of 1975, her body was disintegrating in front of Ron's eyes. She could neither defecate nor walk—

185

she had, on and off, gone through periods in which she could only crawl around—so Ron would hold a Glad Bag under her so she could urinate. She refused medical treatment and became catatonic when Ron insisted they see a doctor. Ron was in the end sympathetic to her stand. She was afraid of completely losing touch with herself in a hospital; with Ron, at least they could see what was going on, though they appeared now to be helpless to stop it. Besides, what would a doctor ever be able to make of her Primaling? He would never understand. They stayed where they were and decided to stick it out.

Ron was grasping for straws. Yet, he thought, if she can just get through this, no matter how bad things are now, she'll come out the other end. He had the distinct sense that a modern, medical miracle was in the making and made plans to write something about it. Meanwhile, Lauren spent eight hours a day in the sound-proofed room. The carpet was covered with half-empty Kleenex boxes.

During the first half of 1975, the strangest thing of all happened. To help relieve Ron of his now terrifying responsibilities, Lauren began calling her older brother Bob, who was at the Primal Institute in L.A., and having Primals with him over the phone. One month, Ron's phone bill was $900. A friend of Lauren's came to New York to "sit" for her. Then Ron's mother arrived from out of town. They were both disastrous experiences. Finally, in February, Bob himself flew in. He built a special Primal box for Ron, so that Ron could find a few minutes' peace now and then by closing himself off from the rest of the apartment: a shell within a shell. Ron was willing to accept anything at this point. Then Bob returned to L.A. and Lauren suddenly sensed that her brother was a murderer. Panicked, she called him in L.A. and asked him if he was a murderer. Bob, perhaps not clear about the question, gave no firm answer. Was he playing a game with her or was he, in fact, a killer? Lauren flew to L.A., heavily drugged for the flight. On her first day there, she called Ron in New York to say that Bob was trying to kill her. Her story seemed cogent to Ron.

Lauren returned to New York where she immediately had vivid Primal memories of Bob killing people. It did not occur to Ron that these "memories" might be another symptom of her mental illness; rather, he concluded that memories of her brother as a murderer unlocked the true source of her illness. And he believed this despite the fact that he knew Bob well and that during the summer of 1973 they had shared a bedroom in L.A. and become friends.

In April of 1975, Ron encountered the friend who had "sat" for Lauren and whom he hadn't seen for almost a year. Ron looked pale, ghostly. He embraced the friend and immediately began to talk about Bob's plan. Bob, he said, had a time schedule for his future crimes. Lauren had discovered that her brother planned to kill her shortly after her twenty-ninth birthday in late May. Ron was slated for death sometime in September. They had already gone to the police, where two detectives took matters into their own hands. It was a measure of Lauren's frantic belief in her own fantasies that she could make others believe them too.

To expedite the investigation, Lauren dictated to Ron a thirty-eight-page typed history of her brother's nefarious past, which she had "recalled." It was a terrifying document; the detectives were solicitous. The manuscript chronologically detailed Bob's crimes, beginning in New Jersey, in the summer of 1950. Lauren was four, Bob six and a half. The two of them are walking home when a puppy jumps up and licks Lauren playfully. "The next thing I know," Lauren wrote, "Bob has grabbed a big stone, then picks up the puppy and starts bashing his head with the stone against some brick surface. He bashes the dog till it's dead and continues to bash it long after, while it twitches spasmodically."

Later that same summer, Lauren reported, Bob in her presence killed a one-year-old child with a shovel that was lying next to the sandbox in which the victim was playing. Then she related another scene from that summer involving three men, masturbation, a murder, and the genesis of Bob's ornate future designs on his sister. This amazing passage, in which Lauren imitated the baby talk of her brother, reads in part: ". . . Moreover, since Jim [one of the three men] killed his own sister when she was 28 because she made him so mad, Bob says he'll kill me by the time I'm 29. . . . I won't ever get more than 29; and if I ever talk about any of this or have a special friend, I could be killed earlier. He further emulates Jim's sexual views on women: 'Womens is for screw—when you growed I can get to screw you. I can screw you when you's dead and I can shoot you up and then screw on you. I seed them shoot up. I know exact how to do it. I'm going to get you on June 2.' "

According to Lauren, Bob had in the past broken all her fingers and her hands and wrists and cut her clitoris. Later, Bob breaks the neck of a girl in Pennsylvania in 1964, then rapes her and Lauren both. Four years alter, Lauren claims, she awakened drugged and bound and was ordered to shoot Bob's girl friend. Lauren refused and Bob retaliated by killing one of Lauren's boy friends.

The document continues to detail labyrinthine plots against Lauren and her friends; they are characterized by drugging, hypnosis, and sensory manipulation to prevent Lauren from remembering the events. At one point, according to the account, Bob told Lauren: "If you ever leave L.A., that's the end of you. Just remember that. If you go to Ron, that's the end of you two."

With the help of addresses and license plate numbers that

Lauren "recalled," the detectives began to work on certain leads in May of 1975. Lauren rested in order to gather strength for her coming testimony against her brother. The police investigated one of the murders, in Cleveland, and were eventually convinced no such crime had taken place. By October they had come up with nothing and they finally suggested to Lauren, whom they had treated with respect, thinking she had been no more than a victim of amnesia at first, that she see the police psychiatrist.

During the interview, Lauren tried to make a fool of the psychiatrist, foiling his attempts to categorize her condition. (Here, once again, as with the detectives and, in a way, with virtually everyone, Lauren was able to summon more than a semblance of normal functioning; she could, during the periods when she was not largely incapacitated, seem compellingly reasonable, poised, and utterly beguiling.) She refused to question the truth of her accusations against Bob. Her existence was built, now more than ever, upon an intricate foundation of paranoid fantasies, and any attempt to threaten the stability of those fantasies met fierce opposition.

Later in October, Lauren and Ron consulted a New York psychiatrist. Lauren succeeded at first in manipulating him too; he was initially impressed with her story and even suggested the two of them write it up. He seemed to accept the fact that they were camped out on the psychotherapeutic frontier. He filled out a sleeping pill prescription for Lauren and did not bother to charge them for the interview. By the second session, however, the psychiatrist seemed to have rethought his original reaction and now showed less indulgence toward Lauren. He directed most of his attention to Ron. Lauren went away bitter, and they never consulted him again.

By November, even Lauren was beginning to find it difficult to believe in her own fantasies any more. She needed solitude and space, so Ron rented an expensive, spacious home in a nearby suburb for her, where she went alone. It was there, at last, that she sensed these remembered "events" couldn't have happened.

"I don't know if anything happened to me any more," she told Ron, frightened, now suspecting even the memories of childhood abuse. Her sister Donna believes the father was "capable of anything" and herself had to ward off his molestations as an adolescent. There seemed little reason, then, to doubt Lauren *was* seriously abused by her father, but even this she began to question.

"What do you mean, you don't know if anything happened to you?" Ron asked angrily. He was almost beyond caring.

"Nancy wanted me to have been raped so badly when I started Primal Therapy that I could feel it in her body. Maybe I just believed what people wanted me to believe." She had needed her fantasies about Bob's murders for complex reasons, no doubt, but it occurred to Ron that one of those reasons might well have been the natural tensions that had grown between Bob and himself as Lauren's rightful protector, a situation that required Lauren to ally herself dramatically with one and viciously to discredit the other.

During November, Lauren became sensitive, almost telepathically, to presences. She would know when someone was standing outside closed doors or had some Pain in the next apartment. She felt "infiltrated by people." Yet Ron, however drained of both energy and solicitude, still hoped that this, finally, was the last hump, and that once Lauren was safely over it, they would at last be able to have a normal relationship.

The first night Lauren spent in the suburbs, though, she began to pick up very bad feelings from Ron, her last ally. Ron felt that everything was lost. Lauren was again suicidal.

She Primaled with Ron and they both felt for an instant that they might—they just might after all this time—be getting clear. After three nights there, she left the house in the suburbs and returned to Ron's apartment closer to the city. Ron forfeited the $1,000 desposit on the house.

On the morning of Friday, November 21, 1975, Lauren told Ron that she wanted to be left alone for the day. He sensed she might kill herself (it was by no means the first time the suspicion arose), but agreed to go off to school, where he planned to sleep that evening in his office. It was hard to walk out of the apartment, but Ron had acceded to far more bizarre wishes than this one. On his way out the door, he made Lauren promise to think of ways to try and change the context of their relationship, to work something out, a better way to Primal, something. "If you promise me that," he said, "I can leave you alone."

Ron arrived at his office at three in the afternoon. By five, he was feeling bad. He was thinking about what they had done wrong. He composed a letter to her, saying that they should spend a certain amount of time apart. They had tried it before, and once again it felt like the right thing to do. He debated whether to return to the apartment. He called a close friend in L.A. who told him to honor his agreement with her. He called his friend again, and this time things seemed more difficult over the phone than they had on the first call. She wanted to be alone, but still, he thought, maybe he ought to go back.

And yet, perhaps at this very moment she was working things out, maybe Primal Therapy was at that very moment coming to an end so that the post-Primal life could begin. He couldn't decide. Even now, she was still manipulating him.

At nine that evening, he drove the mile or so to his apartment. He wasn't supposed to return until eleven the next morning. The bathroom door was closed and the light was on. That had never happened before.

Lauren was lying in the bathtub, drugged. She had looked that way a hundred times before, but now the water was up around her eyes.

Ron wasn't sure at first if she was dead or alive. His heart was pounding so loud and fast that he thought for an instant it might be hers. It was a natural metaphor for their last two and a half years together. He couldn't tell who was who.

Lauren's father wanted to have her buried near his home. But Donna, her sister, decided to have her cremated in New York. The ashes were scattered over the Atlantic Ocean. Her parents did not come up for the occasion.

8. THE FALLACY OF FEELING

Ten days after Lauren's suicide, Ron phoned the friend who had helped him with Lauren. Apart from their encounter the previous spring, they had not spoken with each other for more than a year. He told the friend about Lauren's suicide. For the first time in years Ron's voice was rested. His mourning, paradoxically, was lucid. He began to talk about the closed therapeutic system Lauren and he had operated in. For well over two years, they had lived under the influence of assumptions that now, suddenly, he perceived as false: that she had been doing everything she could already and all they needed were simply better circumstances under which she could continue to Primal; that Primaling would eventually release all her Pain; that it was necessary only for Ron to "cop to" the things Lauren was feeling about him, and not for Lauren likewise to confront any of Ron's suspicions, no matter how persistent.

In specific cases, he felt, it was right to work out her

feelings through Primals, but not as a program. He said it comes down to this: the insidious subtlety of any two or ten or fifty people working together in a closed system, in which an ideology develops that is never germinated from the outside. Primal Therapy, by believing itself to be *the* unique cure for neurosis, may have inhibited those who came to it from bringing much of their own, including their common sense, to bear on its rather simplistic analysis—that "Blocking the Pain produces neurosis," as Janov said, "and feeling the Pain undoes it." Certainly doubts arose at the Institute from time to time, but they were easily overcome by Primal optimism. Perhaps they were training therapists too quickly in order to fill the need, but Primal Therapists nonetheless generally believed themselves to be "the most skilled therapists in the world."

Ron and Lauren's helplessness was compounded by the fact that Lauren herself legislated against receiving outside help by producing somatic symptoms that prevented her from having contact with other people. Ron, too, was locked in by his intense need for a primary relationship at all costs and his consequent fear of leaving her, even for a short time, unless she demanded to be left.

The situation, Ron said, may have been untenable from the beginning. They had been continually involved with what Lauren needed in order to have her next Primal, rather than with the question of whether the whole process of having Primals was in itself useful in the long run.

As for the Primal Therapists who had worked with Lauren in L.A., they couldn't easily see that because of the nature of Primal Therapy it could become for some just another, and perhaps more serious, neurosis, just a histrionic and thoroughly encouraged displacement of feeling. Once, in a group session, a therapists had told a patient who was having trouble feeling the appropriate feelings, "You're really stupid." The remark dented the fellow's armor and he began to cry for the first time in years.

"Tell me again how stupid I am," he said through the tears, "so I can cry some more."

Lauren too, and in a much more elaborate and tragic way, had been led into this fallacy of feeling: that feeling does not involve reason, that emoting is an end in itself. She died a person capable of feeling everything except the limitations of merely feeling.

Obviously, Primal Therapy was not the cause of Lauren's death. The story of her odyssey with Ron is as much about human nature as it is about a specific therapeutic ambience. Also, the story is anomalous; she is by no means a typical "case" nor is she typical of what happens to any distressed person who undergoes a primal-type therapy. Indeed, Primal Therapy has been effective for many people.

But what stands out about Primal Therapy is this: Its fixation on a total cure, and the mythology of the post-Primal person, led it away from a careful diagnosis of individual problems and the idea of therapeutic compromise to a sometimes naïve, simplistic belief in its own omnipotence. In a sense, Primal Therapy was guilty of narcissism on an institutional scale. Of course, for some or maybe most patients, Primal Therapy was no less helpful because of this. One former patient wrote in an issue of the *Journal:* "I like being around people who aren't totally enveloped in the 'Primal consciousness.' After two and one half years of your own Pain, who wants to eat, breathe, and think nothing but Primal gospel? . . . I don't feel that being a 'post-Primal person' makes me a freak in the outside world. I think that that's part of the beauty of Primal Therapy. The therapy is different for everyone—it doesn't turn out a stereotyped post-Primal person who is predictably one thing or another."

A second, very troubling aspect of the therapy is its neo-infantilism. It purports to remove from the therapeutic process what certain critics find most threatening about traditional psychotherapy—the therapist's arrogating to himself the interpretive power to tell a patient what he might actually be feeling (of course, the patient *is* the authority, but largely in an unconscious or preconscious sense; the patient produces all the material for his own cure, but he cannot always produce the cure). In reality, however, Primal Therapy, while contending that it is anti-authoritarian by being anti-intellectual about psychology, is tyrannical on an emotional level. Patients are made to feel that they rarely know what they are up to in the present by therapists eager to anchor *all* of a patient's utterances securely in the infantile past. Furthermore, criticisms voiced by patients about their therapists or the therapy are usually interpreted as projections of "old feelings." This resembles in a way the device used in *est* by which any complaint about the orgianization or its doctrine (or anti-doctrine) is interpreted as just more evidence that the individual does not yet get "It" or understand the game of life.

Still, what explains the behavior of Ron, who in so many other ways is rational, sensitive, and intelligent? What odd crack in his character, what fatal gullibility or cramped need, could account for his intense involvement in Primal Therapy? Ron himself offers a series of explanations, beginning with the fact that to a person eager to straighten out his life, "Primal Therapy seemed right to me. I took it at face value that Janov and Marvin Elder and all the people in Janov's books *had* gone through this process." He had at one time even "idolized" therapists at the Institute. But why, and what was responsible for his blind faith? "I have a certain kind of honesty," Ron says. "I'm very sensitive to the possibility that I'm screwing up, that I'm doing something wrong. It can be a good trait, but if I'm with somebody who's actu-

ally abusing my honesty it can be very bad. I'm always looking at how *I'm* screwing up, not *them*. I just assumed the
Institute knew what it was doing. Similarly, I assumed
Lauren knew what she was doing too. Until she stopped
believing her own Primals I believed that the problem was
the circumstances or the world, and not her."

But why, even after Ron had become so involved, did he
refuse to acknowledge the lunacy of his situation with Lauren and seek outside help? Why did he still think it would
work out? Ron answers with a metaphor: "Say that you're
waiting for a bus. Well, how long do you wait before you
leave? You could wait indefinitely depending on how far you
thought the bus could take you.

"If you want to understand fascism, Nazism or any crazy
movement," he goes on, "you can dismiss them as crazy, but
that doesn't explain *why* people get involved. Well, it happened to me and I'm actually a relatively stable person. It
can happen to anyone if circumstances are right. And they
were for me. Fortunately, I had a way out at the end. Lauren
didn't, except by killing herself."

And then there are the Primal personalities. "You can't
imagine how seductive Marvin and Ilene Elder were to me at
first," Ron says. "They were hard to resist."

Now out in Kansas City, the Elders run the Certified Primal
Therapists' Center, which they claim has been enormously
successful. They talk freely of their therapeutic triumphs,
such as one severely crippled arthritic who got up and walked
normally after a short term of their therapy. Despite their
defection from Janov's camp a few years ago, there are more
similarities than differences between their work and Janov's.
Perhaps the biggest difference is that the Elders stress even
more strongly the origins of psychological disorder in intra-
uterine, birth, and preverbal traumas. They are far more in-

terested in deep nonverbal feelings and physical acting-out than in verbal expression, and their own speech, perhaps not surprisingly, is often a vague psychobabble of ultrasensitivity.

Ilene had been Lauren's therapist for a while at the Institute in L.A., and I asked her about Lauren over a Mexican lunch in Kansas City. "Knowing Lauren so well and working with her so long," she said, "I saw she was atypical. As for the murder memories and that stuff, the feeling part of that she was not yet touching because no one was sitting for her that her body could feel open and safe enough for her to drop down into where she had to go to have those feelings verified, that underlying feeling of death. She'd done the dialectic and put it on a symbol out there."

Ilene was right that Lauren's recollections of her brother's crimes were symbolic fantasies. But why weren't all her rape and torture memories subjected to the same scrutiny when she was at the Institute? Why, in fact, were they implicitly believed and perhaps even encouraged? And what is this *place* "where she had to go to have those feelings verified?" Is there really a special place where, once installed, the patient can meet the Pain head on and then expunge it? The danger of this kind of thinking is that it always gives the therapist an excuse. In Lauren's case, for instance, she met the Pain but the Pain won out. The Primal explanation is this: Lauren was not in the right Pain or the right place, she was only in second- or third-line Pain; if she had really dropped down into that first-line Pain, she would have been able to vanquish it. The solution is too simplistically conceived, the language too mechanical.

There is in Primal Theory this idea that if Lauren or any patient can just get *back there* or *down there* to some Deep Feeling in the past, then recovery naturally follows. But such traumatic and cathartic theories have been generally abandoned for one very good reason. It is widely understood by psychiatrists and psychoanalysts that a trauma does not remain sequestered in the past, like a piece of baggage left in a bus station locker. The human organism adapts to a trauma physiologically and conceptually, and then readapts (the Pain, to use the Primal term, keeps getting expressed in different ways as the individual develops), so that there is no longer a trauma back there in the past *as such*, no longer a discrete Primal Feeling, but rather a succession of adaptive responses to the original trauma. Furthermore, the several traumas of childhood, both large and small, tend to coalesce, the most recent one absorbing the previous ones so that there is as much chance of recovering or reliving some original Primal experience as there is of recovering in pure form from a white sauce the butter, flour, or milk of which it was blended. Traumas can only be understood in the light of an examination of their multiple representations.

If this is true, then what a Primal patient is doing when he Primals a past Pain is reliving only an aspect of it. And even then, it may well be a fantasy or partial fantasy mixed up with a lot of present needs and wishes—one element in a system of meanings, not necessarily an actual event. In short, the process by which one recaptures and "relives" old feelings and works them through is far more complex than Janov's theory suggests, and Janov's theory is neither proved nor completely disproved by the experience of his clients. Had the complexity been recognized in Lauren's case, she and Ron might not have been so readily seduced into a futile search for post-Primaldom.

The Elders seemed so confident, well-meaning, and loving that it is not hard to imagine people trusting them implicitly. Yet what they said at times made little sense.

"The feeling is real," Ilene said, "and until they drop down into that Primal place, patients can't re-experience the true depth of a particular event."

198

But how could one be sure whether a patient was in that Primal place or just doing a good hysterical imitation of being there? If, I asked, a patient Primaled that his father had murdered someone when the patient was four years old, would the Elders be inclined not to question the veracity of it, but instead just deal with the associated feeling? For, important as feelings are, it is also important for a psychotherapist at some juncture in the therapy to challenge what he or she suspects of being fantasy and to try to get at what that fantasy represents. I had in mind not only Lauren, but an anecdote told me by a psychoanalyst who had worked at a VA hospital during World War II where a soldier, under the influence of sodium pentothol, acted out the entire battle of Iwo Jima on the ward floor. Only later was it discovered that he had never left the continental United States.

It seemed to me that a susceptibility to psychic sensationalism and a simultaneous failure to acknowledge deceptions was a crucial problem of Primal Theory. It deserved some discussion. But Marvin only became extremely irritated with my questioning.

"You're asking the question from off to some side and as a result your question hurts," he said. "You're trying to get at something. It's like a jolt, and I feel it's like you've got a slant. [Of course I was trying to get at something and of course I had a slant! Was the post-Primal person beyond even opinion?] It's soaking into your questions. So I feel impelled when I'm trying to respond to deal with that before I start talking. It's like I can't answer your questions in terms of how you ask them."

It went on like this for a while in the restaurant. I explained to him that if I asked the question in *his* terms, I really couldn't ask it at all, and therefore could not get what I considered to be an answer.

"What I sense," I finally told them, "what I get from both

of you, is what comes across often in Janov's books: that only *you* know what a feeling is; that I can't possibly understand the depth of feelings. Tell me," I said, "do you think I've ever had a Deep Feeling?"

"I think you have," Ilene murmured softly. "I feel it in your face."

"Well, *if* you have," Marvin said, "I don't think it's below a certain point."

"Well, I believe you have," Ilene went on. "Just when I was talking to you, did you know that you were starting to have a feeling come up?"

Indeed I did know. Among the many feelings about to come up was the urge to flog them both with the half-eaten burrito on my plate. Although, actually, it was my mother I wanted to flog with my half-eaten burrito, but she was a thousand miles away at the moment. In fact, it wasn't a half-eaten burrito at all that I wanted to use. . . .

I roused myself from my reverie and pressed on: "The feeling I get from Janov's writing, and that I get from both of you, is that you really can't talk to me until you're sure I understand what a feeling is, and so until you're sure you don't want to address the *content* of what I say."

This was, needless to say, an increasingly fruitless discussion. Marvin finished off the lunch with a flourish of psychobabble: "But I do want to address it, that's why I'm bothering. Do you want to work it through so we really hear each other? Then we get to the meaty stuff. I want more than anything to really get down inside, to get *to* it. Then we can get down and talk as deep as I really want to. It would feel good to me if we could just talk freely back and forth and I would feel comfortable and you, too, that we both really know what we're saying, because words get bandied about."

His sententiousness reminded me of a line from Janov's

work: "I am not the one who is intolerant; it is the Primal hypothesis. The truth is highly intolerant of untruths."

I had begun lunch as an interviewer and was concluding it as the Elders' uncooperative Primal patient. They could scarcely distinguish between me as a writer in pursuit of information and me as a member of the Non-Feeling World Out There unwittingly offering them glimpses of my Primal Pool of Pain. They only had a feeling for feeling. They had no feeling for social context, nor for the fact that I had not flown out to Kansas City simply to be subjected to their proud demonstrations of emotional superiority. The paradox was arresting: they were so vigilant about Primal feelings poking their noses through the fence of conversation and behavior (and there is no denying that people *are* constantly divulging important information about themselves) that they had no sense of emotional nuance, of the small shadows that keep falling across dialogue.

Back in L.A., the Primal Institute is still working hard to demonstrate that Primal Therapy is indeed the cure for neurosis. But the impression given by the most recent Primal Therapy brochure is that the Institute has shifted its emphasis away from the primacy of screaming. A research program at the Primal Foundation is now concerned with determining what a Primal is and how much effect it has. Janov has enlisted the aid of a young neurologist to help establish a scientific footing for his theories. By measuring vital signs at various stages in a patient's progress, the neurologist believes he is indicating "the amount of access to Pain." One gets the feeling that the degree to which one is post-Primal will soon be quantifiable and there will then be no question as to who is truly "in touch with his feelings."

The scientificity of the research is dubious, since changes

in vital signs—blood pressure, core body temperature, EEG, EKG—can be responses to any number of phenomena, including the social environment at the Institute, and by themselves mean very little. Perhaps what Arthur Janov said in a speech to a Santa Cruz audience in 1975 is more significant: "Early in Primal Therapy," he commented, "we found that sometimes we took the crutches away from people with too much first-line Pain and got some severely disturbed patients. Now we know better."

CONCLUSIONS

O NCE UPON A TIME, you sought out a psychotherapist because you hadn't slept well in three years, because every time you entered an elevator you almost blacked out from fright, because for some medically inexplicable reason your right arm kept going numb on you, because you couldn't keep the thought out of your mind that Bert Parks was sleeping with your wife, because you couldn't stand it if the vegetables were touching the potatoes on your dinner plate, because there was some impolite secret whispering itself in your ear, because you had this feeling, something not quite specific, yet—well, in fact, to be honest, you hadn't left your house in six months. Eager to remove these obstacles so that you could get on with your life, you spent some time with a therapist and, if you were at all lucky, you found that symptoms began to disappear and all kinds of awful feelings got their chance to be heard, and you tried to talk them out and find your way back into the grim past, and it was a very messy business for a while, you kept blacking out in elevators —though less often now—and new symptoms intruded like uninvited guests, and then you stopped blacking out in elevators altogether—and you hadn't even been discussing elevators!—but other anxieties mounted and you had to adjust to new conceptions of yourself and talk *that* out, and things improved—gradually—and you perhaps came to understand that your life was not as bad as you had thought—the world was not modeled on your family after all—but neither were things ever going to be as good as you would like; yet, in the course of your therapy you had acquired new compassion for yourself and others and at the same time sharpened your critical perspective, and you felt sadder but wiser and you had bought some time to enjoy life without having your right arm go numb in the middle of the day. You had exchanged some of that old neurotic misery for some ordinary human suffering.

These days, fewer seem willing to settle for anything so quaint as ordinary human suffering. Consumer expectations have risen, demanding the "permanent and uninterrupted bliss" offered by Theta, Primal Therapy's post-Primaldom, the you you never thought you could be, a total eclipse of anxiety. The idea of being "cured" has been fetishized; mental health is thought of less and less as the capacity to confront, explore, and transmute the sometimes irreducible contradictions of living, and more and more as a total triumph over all that threatens the autonomy of the individual.

"The Life Institute is an essence thing," I'm told by a man

named Billy. He was raised on a Midwestern farm by his grandmother and his mother, who had been divorced from his father when Billy was four. Nurtured entirely by women, he eventually discovered that he was afraid of girls his own age. He didn't date. He couldn't even approach girls and talk to them. These inhibitions persisted into his thirties, when he took the Life Institute course, a four-and-a-half day, $650 intensive encounter training.

Billy, who now works for the Life Institute, says it showed him how to be himself. "Now I can go up to any girl I want to on the street and begin talking to her. Just a few days ago, I saw a really nice girl in front of Lord and Taylor and I went up and talked to her."

Had his relationships with women improved? "I'm not going with a girl right now, but I know six women and I could marry any of them and I'm sure it would work out. I just know it would work," he smiles with the ominous bravado of a boy poised on the garage roof, all set to prove he can fly. "I have faith."

It is possible to see a number of things in the shift of therapeutic expectations. What the emerging psychological sensibility of the seventies expresses is neither arrogance nor cautious optimism, but instead an eerie pantomime of self-confidence. The revival of positive thinking is almost poignant. Consciousness has been reduced by certain popular dogmas to a psychobabbling subjectivity that legitimizes the passing sensation, the available comfort, the half-truth. Nietzsche spoke of those "who require the belief in a 'free subject' able to choose indifferently, out of that instinct of self-preservation which notoriously justifies every kind of lie." It is a belief that "makes it possible for the majority of mankind— i.e., the weak and oppressed of every sort—to practice the sublime sleight of hand which gives weakness the appearance of free choice and one's natural disposition the distinction of merit."

The psychobabbler of the seventies, clutching his ethos of "that's your space," may indeed be expressing a generosity that had receded in the sixties, but his libertarianism can as easily serve to mask his painful fear of differences as to express his understanding of and equanimity before them. Psychobabble is an idiom in which it is increasingly difficult to indicate either satisfaction or dissatisfaction; it resembles the tranquilizing political rhetoric of campaign promises more closely than it does the medium of honest exchange it purports to be. It is a mode of confession that confesses nothing with a price on its head; it is, to use the phrase of French psychoanalyst Jacques Lacan, *le mot vide*—empty words.

As sociologist Richard Sennett has noted, this empty confessionalism has to some extent been institutionalized at a clinical level. The training therapist, he writes, "is convinced that to treat another human being with respect, he must match whatever is revealed to him with a similar experience of his own. This shows that he 'understands,' that he 'sympathizes.' In fact, this card game leads neither to understanding nor sympathy; if he is any good, the trainee starts over with the knowledge that real respect for other human beings involves a respect for human differences. Such a therapist is increasingly in a minority, however, as the marketing of self-revelation appears in encounter groups, 'T' groups, and the like."

The cultural obsession with "relating" and being "up front" shows itself in the obliviousness to, or plain dismissal of, transference as the key to therapeutic work. Transference can only develop between a therapist and patient when the former refrains, at least initially, from being a "friend" to the latter, withholding aspects of his private life and keeping his own impulses at bay so that the patient may begin to project onto the therapeutic relationship features of his childhood alliances. But transference, even when it develops in therapies such as *est*, co-counseling, Theta, and Primal Therapy, goes relatively unacknowledged; to acknowledge it fully would mean confronting the fact that one's personality is substantially the extension and distortion of formative relationships in the past and not a new "you" available fresh off the rack. Disturbing behavior, unwanted feelings, and destructive impulses are perceived by these therapies simply as accessories to the self. You just sort of work off the problem like a wedding ring that hasn't been removed in years and— *voilà!*—you are psychologically single again, free of old attachments.

But this shift of expectations also indicates that psychotherapeutic and spiritual objectives have increasingly merged and blurred. This confusion is partly the result of the influx of Eastern mysticism to America, partly the residue left by Jung's religious psychology and by many of the neo-Freudians and humanist psychologists who exalted the self and its limitless potential. Then came the newer therapies of transcendence to help pry the issue of psychological self-awareness away from its foundation in the examination of the individual's own history and ease it onto a spiritual plane. British family therapist A. C. Robin Skynner has described the confusion well. If psychological and spiritual endeavors are in fact quite distinct, he argues, "then forms of psychotherapy that confuse them could be much more harmful to the possibility of spiritual development than those that do not recognize the existence of the traditions at all. Thus I believe that the ideas offered by such people as Maslow, Fromm, Rogers, and many leaders of the encounter movement may as easily hinder as help people toward a recognition of their actual position. . . . Because they mix the levels, they stand in danger of offering a half-truth sufficiently like the real thing to satisfy this deep hunger without leading to anything more real and even . . . of simply increasing the attachment to the ordinary self. . . .

"This is why when I cannot find a good eclectic psychotherapist (in the sense of someone who seeks to integrate the best of the different schools) I tend to refer patients to competent Freudian analysts, provided they are agnostic rather than militantly atheistic and demonstrate by the quality of their lives that they are decent and responsible people. For I find that the better Freudians at least have their feet on the ground rather than their heads in the clouds, a good beginning if one wishes to travel reliably along the surface of the earth."

Because of this free mixing of the psychological and the spiritual in popular therapies and popular speech, one often gets a feeling at the best cocktail parties on the enlightenment circuit, or anywhere that people with an appetite for human growth convene: that instead of serving as the medium for human expression, conversation merely refers to that which is inexpressible—the "It" gotten at *est*, the peak experience, the ineffable revelation. Those who agree with Tom Wolfe's assessment of the seventies as the self-promoting "Me Decade" have in a sense not looked deep enough; these people seem barely to be talking about themselves at all. Their words don't belong to them so much as to the current guru of choice or best-selling self-help book. It's as if they've rented their insights for the occasion.

What appears to be occurring in the therapeutic culture of the seventies is the suppression of natural narrative speech itself, the suppression of language in its richest, most associative, most unpredictable, revealing, hence therapeutic form. The erosion of written and spoken English has been widely documented during the last several years, but perhaps nowhere does that damage seem more inhibiting than in the way some people talk—or rather fail to talk—about themselves.

Of course, there is no such thing as a natural ordinary language that is unmediated by external influences; conversely, there is no such thing as psychobabble uninformed by the nuances of ordinary speech. But it makes sense to distinguish between the supple, halting, searching, ordinary speech which at its most alive veers off into common poetry —a way of speaking, that is, which we intuitively know to be fraught with personal meaning seen and unseen—and the prevailing contemporary jargon heavily indebted to fashionable vocabularies promoted by the mass media and giddy therapies. The former is a language we can't quite define (since it seems almost a condition of ordinary language that we don't usually know what we're doing when we speak it), but it expresses something of the history of our existence. The latter has a way of cutting off access to that freer flow of personal history, imagery, memory, and perception in which we can find powerful clues to the origins of our difficulties.

The fact is that the best access most of us have to the meaning of our feelings is through language, and the more flexible that language is the more easily we can get at those meanings. The class of feelings commonly regarded as our inner life cannot be interpreted or understood outside of language. And language here does not mean only spoken language but what goes on in our heads as well—what one could call "inner speech," to use a term the Russian neurologist Alexander Luria has posited for an internalized language function closely associated with, and perhaps identical to, thought. Language also means dreams, of course, whose meaning is revealed to us only when we began to associate verbally on them. Even a psychosomatic symptom is an indication of the body's speaking on our behalf, and only when we talk does the symptom's meaning have a chance of becoming clear.

Memories are not usually traces of past feelings themselves, but traces of our past verbalizations and conceptualizations of past feelings. We may appear to be summoning or re-experiencing past feelings during emotional outbursts but, again, we cannot get a handle on why we have those outbursts unless we have a way of talking about them. But psychobabble, to the extent that it is an idiom isolated in the present, blocks the approach to the past. It is not active language doing its awkward best to point to feelings and meanings, but more like a language frozen in the Lucite of ready-made concepts; it is language that conceals meaning— just another symptom, like the numb right arm. "How shall I see the truth?" asked a young monk. "Through your everyday eyes," replied the Zen master. And one might add that to speak the truth one must use one's everyday language.

The tendency of some of the therapies discussed in this book is to treat feelings as lost or concealed objects. Co-counseling sees "distress" as something on the bottom of your shoe to be scraped off, or as a tape running in your head that can be "discharged." Theta, in the tradition of positive thinking, believes not that problems are to be perceived *through* language but that they are, *in fact*, the actual words spoken, so that talking positively is the way to get rid of "negative mental mass." Primal Therapy felt, perhaps more in its early days than currently, that bad feelings could be objectified as Pain and that Pain was somehow released or resolved through dramatic outbursts characterized by screaming.

But if what one represses is not some objectified feeling that exists independent of the language we use to interpret the world and our lives—but rather the *memory* of a once inadmissible or unpleasant feeling—then looking for feelings can be nothing more than a wild goose chase. To the trained psychotherapeutic listener, those inadmissible feelings are in fact not lost or concealed at all; they are observable in what the patient says and how he says it (word choice, omissions, repetitions, slips, inflection, physical gesture, posture, and other ways). In that sense the unconscious is not a substance or material hidden from view, but is contained in conscious speech itself. One doesn't hide anything so much as simply not look for or recognize it.

What seems to happen in effective psychotherapy (or inspired literature for that matter) is that just enough decorum is waived so that language is not so much spoken as it is finally free to speak itself. It is the design of a good psychotherapeutic context—with its demand for free association, its artful silences—to foster surprises in which the speaker is caught off guard, to give language a chance to point at the person using it. It is when those surprises occur—when the patient is left holding the bag of his own intentions and feelings as expressed by him in *his* language—that the force of the unconscious is felt.

I remember a scene in the movie *The Jimmy Piersall Story* that authentically captured such a moment. Tony Perkins, who played the troubled Boston Red Sox center fielder, is visiting his psychiatrist in the state hospital where he has been sent after breaking down during a baseball game. It is fairly clear to everyone but Tony Perkins at this point that his foremost problem is a father whom he cannot please regardless of what he accomplishes. Afraid, and unable to direct his rage at its source, Piersall/Perkins tries to defend his father against the psychiatrist's probing. In an agitated state, Perkins declares: "But I wouldn't be where I am today if it wasn't for my dad!" The director, respecting the unconscious's *doubles entendres,* imitated a psychoanalytic pause by briefly holding the camera still before panning away.

It is the ultimate effect of too much psychobabble to re-press those surprises during which we start to glimpse the ingenious deceptions of our lives. It is the effect of too much popular talk about "the whole person" and "the autonomous ego" and "the total personality" to repress, with fantasies of self-mastery, the crucial particulars of our frustration. Psychobabble signifies not just the mass caricaturing of insights, but something deeper: the manipulation of language in order to mask the ways that the unconscious often manipulates *us* through language.

The culture is now swimming in quick methods of understanding and changing human behavior. Astrology, Rolfing, biorhythms, iridology, and others are perhaps all effective in their own ways, but the importance of language—that one characteristic that makes us uniquely human—somehow gets lost in the shuffle. A virtue of Freudian theory, for all its shortcomings as practiced in America, is that it points out the extraordinary ordinariness of psychic processes: the structure of our unconscious mental life is preserved in the structure of our natural verbal behavior. Freudianism insists that the monologue which achieves a measure of spontaneity is the best evidence we have for determining what has gone wrong with us. As Lionel Trilling remarked in *Sincerity and Authenticity*: "Its principle of explanation consists in getting the story told—somehow, anyhow—in order to discover how it begins. It presumes that the tale that is told will yield counsel."

Psychobabble represents the rejection of narration in favor of psychological ad copy:

"I'm really into my anger right now," she says.

"That's okay," he replies. "That's your space. Go with the anger."

"Yeah, but I feel a lot of hostility toward you and I feel that I want to get that out."

"That's cool. That's the space you're in. I can understand where you're coming from. I've been there."

"Still, you've really been on my case and I have all this anger that I want to share with you."

"Like I said, that's cool. I want to tell you that I acknowledge your anger and that I acknowledge you."

"Good, I get that it's okay to be angry with you."

The concern is less the treaty than the shape of the negotiating table. True psychobabble has all the intimacy of two PDP-8 computer terminals conversing in an Artificial Intelligence lab, and all in the name of interpersonal relations.

Some people base their rejection of psychoanalysis and traditional psychotherapy on their fear of being manipulated by some "Viennese" concepts as they lie helplessly on a couch or sprawl defenselessly in a chair. That fear is shown for what it is when they then turn to quick "cures" where manipulations of transference and the brandishing of cheap concepts are actually institutionalized. In many popular therapies, the fact remains that jargon is imposed regularly *within* the therapy, as if adopting a new vocabulary is a condition for getting well. (By contrast, a successful traditional therapist is in a position to say that whether you are helped or not by him or her has nothing to do with whether you agree to use an official vocabulary or even whether you agree or are acquainted with the theory that informs the clinical practice. The terminology is employed *outside* of the therapy itself, as an unavoidable convenience that permits therapists to organize and revise their ideas about human behavior, communicate them to other professionals, and put them to a clinical test.)

Est's "getting It" and "what is, is" philosophy, Primal Therapy's visions of post-Primal people, Theta's lingo of rebirth and "affirmations," co-counseling's "Self-Appreciation" all help make human growth into something of a game. Doing so may increase a therapy's effectiveness in the short run, but the danger is that in playing by someone else's rules and time tables, one forfeits the chance to gain any real independence—including independence from therapy—in the long run. In order for quickie therapies like *est* to achieve their "remarkable results," they must provide an engaging vocabulary, indicate a therapeutic goal ("getting It") and, in fact, often bluntly tell you what is wrong with you ("You're all assholes whose lives just don't work"). At work is a very subtle totalitarianism whose therapeutic benefits are received at the cost of relinquishing one's ability to develop more independent judgments about oneself.

There is nothing quick, cheap, or easy about developing judgments about oneself in more traditional psychotherapies, and nothing sure about it either, since all psychotherapies fail often enough; but one's freedom is not as likely to be abridged in the process. For despite the belief in some quarters that what therapists do is *tell* you what is wrong with you, it would be much closer to the truth to say that *you* tell *them* what is wrong with you, whether you always want to or not, and that those revelations usually remain open to a dialectical method of interpretation.

But, of course, traditional psychoanalytic terms and concepts have been absorbed into the mainstream in ways that make them seem every bit as authoritarian as the newest cliché, and even more so considering their venerable status. "Expressions such as repression, defense, return of the repressed, regression, the Oedipus complex, castration anxiety, and, of course, penis envy have become household words," writes Jarl Dyrud of the University of Chicago. "Taken out of context, treated as truths about human nature, they lose their value. For instance, castration anxiety really describes a shrinking genital sensation so well that it is difficult to re-

214

member that this adjective and noun are not literally appropriate but are simply a metaphor for a range of experiences in growing up. The analytic work involves the verbs and adverbs of what is and has been going on rather than mere labeling."

The Freudian terminology that has infiltrated public consciousness has become for many a sort of psychobabble as insidious and inaccessible as any other. The model of psychic processes that Freud proposed drew on terminology belonging to the influential physical sciences in late nineteenth century Europe—terms such as force, energy, cathexis, structure, and drive. The hidden assumption was that one could talk about the psyche as if it were a complex machine whose parts could be examined to see if they were in good working order. That assumption was not seriously challenged until after World War II. At that point, criticisms of Freud's model became more pronounced for reasons reviewed recently by English psychoanalyst Charles Rycroft:

"One was the increasing complexity of the model itself as it became elaborated by theorists like Hans Hartmann who made heroic attempts to reconcile respect for the truth with loyalty to the Freudian model. . . . Another was the influence, greater in England than in America, of Wittgenstein and the linguistic philosophers, which led some analysts to feel that the fallacy of reification was involved in endowing abstract entities such as id, ego, aggression, and sexuality with attributes and propulsive powers and in evoking them as causal explanations.

"A third reason was an increasing awareness of a major discrepancy between theory and practice; theory explained why people did things in terms of causation, while in practice analysts interpreted why their patients did things, even involuntarily, in terms of motive and meaning. A fourth was the influence of existentialism, which drew attention to the self, an agent who actively experienced things and initiated actions, but who could not be located satisfactorily anywhere within the psychic apparatus. And fifth, physics and chemistry ceased to be the sciences which it was natural to use as models for theories about human behavior."

As a result of these forces, people inside and outside of the psychoanalytic movement were growing uncertain. If psychoanalysis kept professing to be a science along the lines of a natural science like physics or chemistry, and it was becoming clear that psychoanalysis could never safely make that claim, then were all of Freud's contributions imperiled—even the concept of a dynamic unconscious, infantile sexuality, the principles of dream interpretation, the therapy itself? Was Freud's clinical baby now in danger of being thrown out with the mechanistic bath water?

Freud himself considered his model and his terminology to be no more than dramatic metaphors; the little Oedipal boy didn't really want to have *intercourse* with his mother, of course, but he did have a deep, understandable, biological and sexual attraction for her whose later consequences he, like Oedipus, was unaware of. The unconscious was of course not something one could dissect in the laboratory, but it was a term for a particular aspect of our mental life. Still, the literal-minded have always wanted to be *shown* the unconscious if they were going to believe that such a thing existed. When no unconscious could be produced for laboratory inspection, the disappointed crowd dispersed to attend behaviorist sideshows where at least the rats could be *seen* in their mazes; or it dispersed to colloquiums on existentialism where all the talk was about the self and the whole person and even if no one could exactly find the self or measure it, well, still, everyone seemed to know what the self was. But who would bother to understand the ever more complex conceptualizations of psychoanalytic theory?

216

Most current popular therapies can be explained partly as attempts to simplify Freudian concepts and pare down the terminology to achieve an accessible, brief procedure for curing "neurotics." In their zeal for results, however, they have abandoned the spirit of psychoanalysis. "Psychoanalysis," Freud once told a patient, "demands a degree of honesty which is unusual and ⌐.en impossible in bourgeois society." But many popular therapies, while touting truth, seem to demand only that degree of honesty which is easily possible in bourgeois society. They don't seem to have digested Freudianism so much as circumvented it; and in the attempt to surmount the sometimes confining vocabulary of Freudianism they have only substituted jargon that has roots in no significant theory at all.

2

Those innovators who have sought to remain largely true to the spirit of psychoanalysis while trying to broaden its impact have had to deal with the many problems of the language of psychoanalysis—the confusing psychoanalese.

Of those newer therapies that have tried to convert psychoanalytic principles into an expedient therapy with a new terminology, Eric Berne's transactional analysis has been among the most successful. Berne, a Freudian-trained analyst, developed transactional analysis in the late fifties following his rejection for membership in the San Francisco Psychoanalytic Institute. He was motivated not only by his exclusion from the brotherhood of orthodox psychoanalysts, which hurt him deeply, but also by a growing disdain for psychoanalysis's obsession with gratuitously complex theory and long-term therapy. Berne was interested in results; "Get well first," one of his credos goes, "analyze later." He was fond of comparing the practice of psychotherapy to poker, one of his personal passions. In a poker game, only winning counts, not coming close. Likewise in therapy, he felt, only curing the patient counts, not progress.

Like the Freudians, Berne was grimly deterministic. He believed that the individual's psychological destiny was established during the first six years of life. People spend their entire lives following a "life script," composed of "transactions" and "games," based on early interaction within the family. To each of those neurotic games Berne assigns a name, such as "Little Old Me," "I'll Show Them," "See What You've Done Now," "Man Talk," "Water Cooler," and on and on.

The individual involved in these games is divided into three parts, the Parent, the Adult, and the Child. Where Freud posited "psychic agencies" in perennial conflict and called them superego, ego, and id, Berne has three "ego states" he calls Parent, Adult, and Child. In the way they are used in TA, Parent, Adult, and Child (PAC) are often synonymous with Freud's superego, ego, and id—the Parent referring basically to the morality acquired from the parents, the Adult referring to the integrated, reality-oriented ego, and the Child to the unruly, instinctual id. But there are differences, for PAC are "complete ego states," each one containing elements of the superego, ego, and id.

Early life experiences determine the relative strength of the three ego states and therefore one's basic "life position." For instance, a person with a strong Child tends to think of himself in adult life as being smaller and less competent than others. His life position is "I'm not O.K.—You're O.K." A person with a Child-Contaminated-Adult with a Blocked-Out-Parent takes the life position "I'm not O.K.—You're not O.K." and might become a criminal psychopath. Using the PAC theme, Berne and his followers are able to cover a lot of psychopathological ground, and one of TA's appeals is clearly the chance to play around with a new and somewhat fanciful vocabulary. Saying of someone that he has a very strong Parent with a Blocked-Out-Child who likes to play the game "Blemish" whose "payoff" is not having to look at how Decommissioned his Adult is sounds much less threatening than calling him a prepsychotic obsessive-compulsive with an authoritarian defense formation, or some such. And, at the same time, it certainly says a lot more than that he's simply hung-up on perfection and uptight on top of it all.

Through the analysis of life scripts performed with the aid of transactional diagrams in small TA groups (which last only about twenty or so sessions), one strengthens the Adult who, understanding that everyone is basically okay, can persuade the Parent and Child to accept its basic life position, that of "I'm O.K.—You're O.K."

TA, carried forward by Thomas A. Harris, Claude Steiner, and others, has been enormously successful. Much of that success has to be attributed to a clever, easy-to-understand terminology that manages to capture enough Freudian theory on the one hand, and enough sheer positivism on the other, to endear TA to a wide range of people and institutions. As for TA theory, there is nothing in it that one can't find in Freud, Adler, Sullivan, drama therapy, and a few others. "In fact," one psychiatrist has observed, "transactional analysis is essentially a language."

Berne breathed neologisms and catchphrases; TA bulges with lists, and words taken from the dictionary of modern culture, all employed in the service of his theories. Compared to TA's manic habit of naming everything ("stroking," "sweatshirts," "trading stamps," "cold fuzzies," etc.), a traditional concept like the Oedipus complex begins to seem refreshingly economical. One observer of TA has remarked that patients in it are "like characters in a TV situation comedy or game show." Indeed, one gets the sense that, however involved TA's roots in depth psychology, the endless labeling and name-calling, though not malicious, is an invitation to see behavior too much as a mechanical game. The TA patient must agree in his "contract" with the therapist to use the TA vocabulary as part of his therapy. Countless interpersonal transactions are ingeniously plotted and named by Berne, but the danger is that patients will come to see themselves simply as combinations of detachable roles and ego states.

TA patients aspire to be the Adult who can honestly say "I'm O.K.—You're O.K.," as if the only desired outcome of emotional growth should be blanket tolerance toward oneself and others, and not also an increased suspicion of appearances. The criticism mounted against psychotherapies in general by the political left, that they merely adjust one to the status quo, applies particularly to TA. By objectifying mature or rational behavior as the Adult with its "I'm O.K.—You're O.K." mentality, TA is suggesting that all problems may be solved on the personal level; what the world needs, TA implies, is just more grown-ups who do not challenge the existing order. The Adult is a specious category; and, given the brevity of the average TA cure, one suspects that this Adult has not completely integrated the Child or Parent but only fixed them with labels and sent them back into their corners.

With TA, Berne, who began as a Freudian, has popularized many Freudian principles but has abandoned psychoanalysis in the process. A psychoanalyst and professor of psychiatry named Roy Schafer, however, has his own ideas about how to excise psychoanalysis's obsolete concepts and repair its sclerotic language without killing the patient. Schafer speaks from within the psychoanalytic establishment and does not endorse quick cures. But while his 1976 collection of essays, *A New Language for Psychoanalysis*, is a defense of psychoanalysis, his ideas about language and psychology address far more general problems in the way we talk about our feelings.

Schafer's proposed "new language" for psychoanalysis is designed to have at least three important effects: to stem the tide of psychoanalytic theories and concepts that divide analysts even when their actual clinical techniques are similar; to substitute for highly technical, cabalistic jargon the use of a more ordinary but systematic language with an even greater potential for clarifying and resolving psychological problems; and, by virtue of its being a more ordinary language, to help reconcile the language of psychoanalytic theory with the language patients and analysts use in practice.

What Schafer suggests with a radical thoroughness is that psychoanalysts adopt the rules of what he calls "action language" to replace the confusing mixture of physicochemical and biological language in Freudian theory. Schafer's primary objection to traditional psychoanalytic explanation is that, by objectifying psychic forces and feelings as things that happen *to* us as opposed to actions that we initiate, consciously or unconsciously, it encourages a "disclaiming" of action, much like many of the therapies discussed in this book.

The tendency of the language of Freud's metapsychology (the theoretical dimension of his psychology) is to regard behavior as being *caused* by something, as in "Your unresolved fixation on mother at an oral stage of development causes you to think of all sexual relationships now as a large breast to suck on for nourishment." But clearly, Schafer argues, neither an external force nor something inside a person *causes* him to think or act that way. It is *he* who is doing the thinking, and thinking is a form of action for which he must take responsibility. People don't have causes; they have motives and meanings for doing what they do and feeling what they feel, and it ought to be the objective of psycho-analysis to make the individual conscious of his own actions without the contradictory use of a language that endows mental processes and feelings with physical properties.

Schafer does not throw out key psychoanalytic concepts. He merely recasts them in verbal and adverbial forms to show that these concepts are not things, but things that we *do*. In the process, Schafer is defining action in the broadest possible sense. Unconscious behavior is action, just in another mode than conscious behavior. Thought is action, even if it has been provoked by unconscious mental processes, for those processes are themselves types of action. Language is action, memory is action, and even emotions are action since, as Schafer writes, "What we call our emotions, far from being simply 'there' as entities of some sort to be thought about, are 'there' only by virtue of a certain kind of thinking."

It is interesting to see how Schafer would translate traditional interpretations into action language:

"It was an old anger you finally got out" becomes "You finally acted angrily after all this time."

"You broke through the internal barriers against your feelings of love" becomes "You finally did not refrain from acting lovingly."

"Your chronic deep sense of worthlessness comes from the condemning inner voice of your mother" becomes "You regularly imagine your mother's voice condemning you, and, agreeing with it, regard yourself as being essentially worthless."

To the ear, it sounds as if what Schafer is gaining in logical consistency he is losing in grace of expression, but once he has rejected the contradictions of metapsychological language he is obliged to make a total revision of that language according to his rules of action language. Otherwise he would be leaving the field open to an even greater mix of linguistic styles and philosophical conceptions. Schafer lays down the law with no sympathy for traditional habits of explanation. For example:

—Feelings are not substances or things but actions and active fantasies pursued by the individual. An emotion doesn't exist "apart from the actions by which we bring it into the world, such as naming, choosing words, gesturing, and observing one's actions."

—There is no such thing as an "old feeling." In action language one would not say "That old feeling has resurfaced" or even "That old black magic has me in its spell" or any locution that treats a feeling as an object. Instead, one would say something like, "I am thinking of some previous situation in more or less the same emotional way as I remember having acted within that situation in its time."

—Feelings don't accumulate or build up inside like pressurized steam or antiques in an increasingly cluttered attic, for those notions postulate "a universe of emotion that is so like a universe of static objects that it cannot convey the flux and the wonder of emotional experience." That is a mistake made in many popular therapies in which old feelings are thought to survive intact from the past, needing only to be released in the present; the consequences of that kind of thinking can be palpable, as with Ron and Lauren's experience in Primal Therapy. It is wrong-headed thinking because it presupposes, in Schafer's words, "a constant or unchanging stimulus and situation as well as a type of action, and as a result we may not realize that (ordinarily within certain limits) the agent might be continuously redefining the stimulus in terms of his or her changing situation."

—There should be no talk of "real feelings" or "true feelings" that implies that those which aren't real or true are therefore not meant, since of course they are also meant, though in a different and unconscious action mode.

—The "self" and "identity" are not facts about a person, or something the person *has*, but "technical ways of thinking about people."

—There is no inexpressible "subjective core," no "feel" to an event that cannot be put into words. Whether we have found those words yet is another matter. Schafer argues that ambiguity and "the correlated prospect of multiple versions is not the same as inaccessibility and inexpressibility." This does not seem to be an argument that we *ought* to put our feelings into words, but rather that all our feelings are potentially expressible in words.

—While it is the business of psychoanalysts to "emphasize action in the unconscious mode, we shall neither engage in speculation about what is ultimately unutterable in any form nor build elaborate theories on the basis of unfalsifiable propositions concerning mental activity at the very beginning of infancy." This statement could be aimed directly at the speculations of Scientology, Primal Therapy, and Theta about the mental processes of the fetus and newborn child, at co-counseling's assumption that there is some natural human condition of zest, or at the emphasis of popular self-help literature on the "real you," etc.

—The words we use to denote emotional states, like love, anger, guilt, happiness, bliss, despair, fear, etc., do not exist in the world as events or properties one has. Schafer writes: "To love and act lovingly are the proper forms of rendering the idea of love in action language. Having thereby lost its status as an entity in this language, love can no longer make the world go round; it can no longer glow, grow, or wither; and it can no longer be lost or found, cherished, poisoned, or destroyed."

Although these examples do not do full justice to the scope of Schafer's thinking in psychology, philosophy, and linguistics, they seem sufficiently revolutionary, even obsessive. But Schafer is not unaware that his critique of metapsychological language seems to serve also as a critique of literature, in that writers use metaphor, personification, apostrophe and other devices to objectify feelings. Literature is not Schafer's concern in the book, but he does remind readers that "a soulful language cannot help us understand all we wish to understand." There is obviously some truth to the idea that our unthinking reliance on habitual expressions can hinder us from seeing our true relationship to our feelings. But while metaphors may conceal, they can also penetrate deeply, and the debts all great psychologists have paid to art and literature confirm this.

So Schafer is very careful to state at the end of *A New Language for Psychoanalysis* that his prescription for action language applies basically to "systematic discourse." He is advocating a better, more consistent way to theorize and write about human behavior than that offered by muddied Freudian metapsychology, but he is not recommending, with a utopian flourish, a new and better way for everyone to talk about themselves. "Because I have concerned myself chiefly with systematic discourse," he writes, "I think I am safe from the charge of advocating the use of a language that will impoverish our existence."

Be that as it may, Schafer is indeed implying at least a better way for psychoanalysts and therapists to talk with their patients. Psychoanalytic theory is not, nor should it be, so divorced from its practice that a profound revision of the former will have no effect on the techniques of the latter. In fact, Schafer is quick to defend himself against the counter-criticism that he is dealing *only* with theory by saying, "I have consistently couched my discussion in terms that apply directly to psychoanalytic interpretation or could do so with only a little modification."

Of course, the notion that the rules of Schafer's action language might somehow be implemented in normal everyday speech is wildly audacious, and if Schafer or anyone else thought such a plan would succeed, we could indeed accuse him or her not only of "advocating the use of a language that will impoverish our existence," but of wishful thinking as well.

Schafer's proposal is difficult, ambitious, and provokes some disturbing issues about language and psychology. It remains to be seen what the psychoanalytic or psychological establishments make of his ideas. In any case, however, one importance of his proposal is that it takes seriously the dependence of self-understanding on language—"In psychoanalysis," he writes, "the words *are* the understanding." Overly fastidious though he may be, Schafer points helpfully away from enlightenment through ethereal self-regarding and back to self-awareness, psychological responsibility, and the central importance of language.

3

"It is one of our problems," Lewis Thomas wrote in *Lives of a Cell*, "that as we become crowded together, the sounds we make to each other, in our increasingly complex communication systems, become more random-sounding, accidental or incidental, and we have trouble selecting meaningful signals out of the noise. One reason is, of course, that we do not seem to be able to restrict our communication to information-bearing, relevant signals. Given any new technology for transmitting information, we seem bound to use it for great quantities of small talk."

Consider for a moment a society in which psychobabble has become what passes for ordinary language. Anyone left in this society with an ear for nuance and a sense of history would have a harder and harder time trying to elicit what used to be called meaning from the reign of platitudes. Wittgenstein understood that the limits of language are the limits of one's world. Linguist Edward Sapir flatly observed, "The fact of the matter is that the 'real world' is to a large extent unconsciously built up on the language habits of the group." If what these men say about language and the real world is true, then the ascendancy of psychobabble would indicate that the modern range of experience, far from being expanded, had been diminished by the prevalence of verbal labels. In a world dominated by psychobabble, everyone would be getting their empty heads together in the intolerably banal here and now. Everyone would be engaged in a sort of perpetual emotional filibuster unconsciously designed to prevent any real issues from coming to a vote.

On second thought, don't consider it. It's an unwarranted luxury to invent an adversary when the "noise" is already real enough. Gossip has begun to usurp the place of literature. Autobiography has replaced ideology. The "inner" life has absorbed much of the little that is left of collective public life.

It will probably all go away eventually, at least for a while. At some future time, the seventies will have receded sufficiently so that historians may safely write that *est*, Theta, Primal Therapy, and others represented just another historical instant in which the strands of mind cure religion and secular psychotherapy intertwined and caught people in visions of unlimited potential and divine contentment.

Already there seem to be some signs of a denouement in the drama. One could be wrong about it—what happened one night in early 1977 a few miles outside of Boston may not, in the end, signal a loss of momentum or hint at some approaching decadence, but there was still something very peculiar and very fey about it. About twenty people gathered in a small house to hear about a new (although it had been developing for many years) discipline called Mind Freedom from three of its followers. Those who attended that night had already spent varying amounts of time, energy, and money in the pursuit of personal truth and, still unsatisfied, had converged here like people on the last leg of a scavenger hunt. Billy, the employee of the Life Institute who a few months earlier had told me that there were six women he could marry and be happy with any one of them, was there, eager to discover what Mind Freedom knew that the Life Institute did not. A couple of rebirthers had come, one of whom was doing double duty as an advanceman for Mind Freedom. Several in attendance had been through *est*, their presence implying that "getting It" had not been enough.

The keynote speaker, a young man from New York sporting Earth Shoes and a cadmium red chemise Lacoste, referred often during his long introductory remarks to his previous experiences in *est* and rebirthing. *Est*, he said, forced you to ask questions; but in Mind Freedom, you didn't need to ask any questions. Theta, with its "affirmations," taught you to replace your "negative programs" with "positive ones"; but in Mind Freedom, he said, you learned to "let go of *all* programs." Rebirthing, a process he had undergone numerous times, was helpful, but "there was a spillover," and the whole thing forced you to confront old feelings; but in Mind Freedom, he said, there was no need to confront old feelings, or even present ones for that matter.

With Mind Freedom, he said, "I feel like I've finally come home." He had been in it for fourteen weeks.

So what did it do, this thirty-hour, $250 course? What it did, said the keynote speaker, was teach you to let go. If something bothered you, you just let it go—anger, anxiety, apathy, frustration, the whole works. "The Mind Freedom method," I had read earlier in the promotional material, "is enjoyable, effortless and practical. It requires no unpleasant confrontation or re-experiencing. Most of the time we express, suppress or escape our feelings. Mind Freedom offers another alternative—*release!* . . . Using this method, one can achieve any goal effortlessly, including the goal of total freedom."

But how did it work? Trying to explain that, replied a female representative of Mind Freedom, echoing *est*, "would be like trying to describe the taste of an orange to someone who had never tasted one." Did you have to believe in it in order for it to work? Not really.

But there was no question that it worked. The mother of the keynote speaker had taken Mind Freedom. Then the sprinkler system in her apartment burst and damaged everything. At first she got tense—she was an interior decorator by trade on top of it all—but then she called her son, who reminded her how to let go. She let go. Coolly she called the insurance company and sent the rug out to be cleaned. That was one example of how Mind Freedom worked. Another was offered by the rebirther who now doubled as a Mind Freedom rider. He had been driving alone late one night from New York to Boston and he got tense behind the wheel. Driving often made him tense. Then he let go, and the rest of the trip was a breeze.

At the end of the two-hour discussion, one woman, who had sat in a reverent stupor for the entire time without talking or asking any questions, suddenly raised her hand and said, "I feel complete about Mind Freedom. When can I sign up?"

Where could psychobabble go from here? Mind Freedom had to be the last word in popular therapy—a movement with no expressible theory, no goal beyond a meditative letting go. The actual thirty-hour process would itself probably amount to something, and people with a primed capacity for faith would surely find their temporary salvation here. But no eventual therapeutic triumph could possibly cure the lethargy of its clients. In many ways they were like steady car customers who, having purchased a Plymouth each of the last ten years, were quite obviously going to buy another one regardless, but who still required the desultory formality of kicking a few tires in the showroom before writing the check.

Their talk was aimless, giving the impression that they had hired themselves out to a glib vocabulary, that they were looking for themselves where they didn't live. What was at stake that evening was not, in the end, the effectiveness of a particular therapy or even "happiness" so much as the survival of curiosity, healthy ambivalence, contradiction, what the Hassidics once called "holy insecurity."

Art critic Harold Rosenberg once defined intellectuals as those who turn answers into questions. Those who have a passion for doing the opposite soon forget they had questions in the first place. The problem is not that so many are constantly looking for enlightenment these days, but that so many are constantly finding it.

SELECTED
BIBLIOGRAPHY

Alexander, Frank B., and Selesnick, Sheldon T., *The History of Psychiatry*. New York, 1966.

Becker, Ernest, *The Denial of Death*. New York, 1973.

Berne, Eric, *Games People Play: The Psychology of Human Relationships*. London, 1966.

————, *Beyond Games and Scripts*. New York, 1976.

Bry, Adelaide, *The Sexually Aggressive Woman*. New York, 1975.

————, *est: 60 Hours That Transform Your Life*. New York, 1976.

Cannel, Ward, and Macklin, June, *The Human Nature Industry*. New York, 1973.

Colby, Kenneth Mark, *Artificial Paranoia: A Computer Simulation of Paranoid Processes*. New York, 1975.

Crews, Frederick, *Out of My System: Psychoanalysis, Ideology, and Critical Method*. New York, 1975.

Evans, Christopher, *Cults of Unreason*. New York, 1973.

Fosdick, Harry Emerson, *On Being a Real Person*. New York, 1943.

Frederick, Carl, *est: Playing the Game the New Way*. New York, 1974.

Freud, Sigmund, *The Standard Editio·¹ of the Complete Psychological Works of Sigmund Freud*. London, 1953.

Gardner, Martin, *Facts and Fallacies in the Name c̣ Science*. New York, 1957.

Hargrove, Robert A., *est: Making Life Work*. New York, 1976.

Harris, Thomas A., *I'm O.K.—You're O.K.* New York, 1967.

Hubbard, L. Ron, *Dianetics: The Modern Science of Mental Health*. New York, 1950.

Jackins, Harvey, *The Human Situation*. Seattle, 1973.

———, *The Human Side of Human Beings: The Theory of Re-evaluation Counseling*. Seattle, 1965.

———, *Quotes from Harvey Jackins*. Seattle, 1975.

Fundamentals of Co-counseling Manual. Seattle, 1962.

Jacoby, Russell, *Social Amnesia: A Critique of Conformist Psychology from Adler to Laing*. Boston, 1975.

Janov, Arthur, *The Primal Scream*. New York, 1970.

———, *The Primal Revolution*. New York, 1972.

———, ed., *The Journal of Primal Therapy*, Vol. 1, No. 1 (1973) through Vol. 2, No. 4 (1975).

Kovel, Joel, *A Complete Guide to Therapy*. New York, 1976.

Lacan, Jacques, "The Insistence of the Letter in the Unconscious," in Jacques Ehrmann, ed., *Structuralism*. New York, 1970.

Lasch, Christopher, "The Narcissistic Society," in *The New York Review of Books* (Sept. 30, 1976).

Liebman, Joshua Loth, *Peace of Mind*. New York, 1946.

Marcuse, Herbert, *Eros and Civilization: A Philosophical Inquiry into Freud*. Boston, 1955.

Marin, Peter, "The New Narcissism," in *Harper's Magazine* (Oct., 1975).

Mitchell, Juliet, *Psychoanalysis and Feminism: Freud, Reich, Laing and Women*. New York, 1974.

Meyer, Donald, *The Positive Thinkers: A Study of the American Quest for Health, Wealth and Personal Power from Mary Baker Eddy to Norman Vincent Peale*. New York, 196ƒ.

Rieff, Philip, *The Triumph of the Therapeutic: Uses of Faith After Freud*. New York, 1966.

Schafer, Roy, *A New Language for Psychoanalysis*. New Haven, 1976.

Schur, Edwin, *The Awareness Trap: Self-Absorption Instead of Social Change*. New York, 1976.

Smith, Adam, *Powers of Mind*. New York, 1975.

Solomon, Robert C., *The Passions: The Myth and Nature of Human Emotion*. New York, 1976.

Steiner, Lee R., *Where Do People Take Their Troubles?* Boston, 1945.

Trilling, Lionel, *Sincerity and Authenticity*. Cambridge, Mass., 1971.

Viscott, David, *Feel Free: How to Do Everything You Want Without Feeling Guilty*. New York, 1971.

———, *How to Make Winning Your Lifestyle: A Psychiatrist's Guide to Getting and Keeping the Upper Hand*. New York, 1972.

———, *How to Live With Another Person*. New York, 1974.

———, *The Language of Feelings*. New York, 1976.

Weizenbaum, Joseph, *Computer Power and Human Reason: From Judgment to Calculation*. San Francisco, 1975.

Richard Dean Rosen was born in Chicago, grew up in Highland Park, Illinois, and attended Brown and Harvard Universities. He has since taught writing at the latter. Now living in the Boston area, Mr. Rosen has served as arts editor, books editor, and restaurant columnist for the Boston Phoenix *and currently reviews restaurants for* Boston Magazine. *His first book,* Me and My Friends, We No Longer Profess Any Graces: A Premature Memoir, *was published when he was still an undergraduate.*